NEW DIRECTIONS FOR CHILD DEVELOPMENT

William Damon, *Brown University*
EDITOR-IN-CHIEF

D0932639

Narrative and Storytelling: Implications for Understanding Moral Development

Mark B. Tappan
Colby College

Martin J. Packer
University of Michigan

EDITORS

Number 54, Winter 1991

JOSSEY-BASS INC., PUBLISHERS, San Francisco

MAXWELL MACMILLAN INTERNATIONAL PUBLISHING GROUP
New York • Oxford • Singapore • Sydney • Toronto

University of
Wisconsin-Madison
Libraries

NARRATIVE AND STORYTELLING: IMPLICATIONS FOR
UNDERSTANDING MORAL DEVELOPMENT
Mark B. Tappan, Martin J. Packer (eds.)
New Directions for Child Development, no. 54
William Damon, Editor-in-Chief

Microfilm copies of issues and articles are available in 16mm and 35mm,
as well as microfiche in 105mm, through University Microfilms Inc., 300
North Zeeb Road, Ann Arbor, Michigan 48106.

LC 85-644581   ISSN 0195-2269   ISBN 1-55542-770-7

NEW DIRECTIONS FOR CHILD DEVELOPMENT is part of The Jossey-Bass
Education Series and is published quarterly by Jossey-Bass Inc., Publish-
ers (publication number USPS 494-090). Second-class postage paid at
San Francisco, California, and at additional mailing offices. POSTMASTER:
Send address changes to Jossey-Bass Inc., Publishers, 350 Sansome Street,
San Francisco, California 94104.

EDITORIAL CORRESPONDENCE should be sent to the Editor-in-Chief,
William Damon, Department of Education, Box 1938, Brown University,
Providence, Rhode Island 02912.

Cover photograph by Wernher Krutein/PHOTOVAULT © 1990.

Printed on acid-free paper in the United States of America.

CONTENTS

EDITORS' NOTES

The past decade has witnessed dramatic changes in the field of moral development theory and research; most of these changes have arisen from critiques of, and challenges to, the paradigm that has dominated the field for more than thirty years: Lawrence Kohlberg's (1969, 1981, 1984) cognitive-developmental approach. While researchers and practitioners interested in the moral lives of human beings owe an enormous debt to Kohlberg—and to the power of his vision—for single-handedly bringing the study of moral development into the mainstream of psychology and education, there is a growing awareness of the metatheoretical, theoretical, and methodological limitations of his approach. We believe that among the many and varied critiques of, and challenges to, Kohlberg's work, the most significant are based on the argument that the cognitive-developmental attempt to formally reconstruct the ontogenesis of moral competence, via the postulation of a cross-culturally universal sequence of six structurally defined stages of justice reasoning, does not sufficiently acknowledge the multidimensional nature of the moral domain; does not adequately capture the cognitive, affective, and conative complexity of individuals' real-life moral experiences; and does not acknowledge the profound ways in which contextual factors, including differences in gender, race, class, and culture, shape the meaning of those experiences to individuals.

The aim of this volume, *Narrative and Storytelling: Implications for Understanding Moral Development,* is to present a set of new, interdisciplinary approaches to the study of moral development that attempts to respond to these concerns. These approaches share a common focus on narrative (storytelling) as a central aspect of human existence, based on the premise that we are, by our very nature, "story-telling animals"—that we understand our actions, and the actions of others, primarily through narrative (MacIntyre, 1981). The function of narrative is thus to endow a certain sequence of events with meaning, particularly *moral meaning* (White, 1981); hence these approaches all assume that narrative provides a uniquely powerful vehicle for understanding human experience, especially human *moral experience.*

What else do these narrative approaches to moral development have in common? First, they share an appreciation for the multifaceted character of the moral domain, reflecting on an awareness that there are many different moral stories that can be, and are, told about the moral lives of human beings. Second, they share an interest in lived moral experience as it occurs in the time, space, and relational contexts of everyday life, given that these are the primary dimensions of narrative. Third, they all privilege language and culture as fundamentally constitutive of meaning and thus assume that moral thoughts, feelings, and actions are mediated by words, utterances, and forms of discourse. Moreover, it is because thoughts, feelings, and actions are semantically structured in this way that narrative—as a specific genre of discourse—is a primary mode by which meaning is made. Finally, all of the approaches in this volume share a methodological interest in the "problem of interpretation"—that is, in the ways in which researchers interpret and understand the meaning of others' moral experiences—and they call for researchers to acknowledge the ways in which their own prejudices, assumptions, and moral commitments influence and underpin their understanding of others' moral stories. Each chapter in this volume, therefore, highlights a way in which a focus on narrative, and an appreciation of these complex and complicated issues, leads to a new approach to the study of moral development, and, by extension, to the practice of moral education.

In the first chapter, Mark B. Tappan examines the process by which individuals come to claim authority and assume responsibility for their moral thoughts, feelings, and actions. He explores the primary link between narrative and moral experience and considers the parallels between authoring a novel and authoring a narrative of lived experience. Drawing on the work of Mikhail Bakhtin, Tappan suggests that the development of moral authority is enhanced when individuals are able to make the words of others their own, to speak in "internally persuasive" forms of discourse, and hence to "author"—and thus "authorize"—stories about their own lived moral experiences.

James M. Day, in the second chapter, argues that narrative and dramatic processes may, in fact, mediate and shape both moral "judgment" and moral "action," two concepts that have been central to the study of moral development. In particular, he outlines the notion of the "moral audience," in front of which individuals seem to rehearse, review, and redefine their moral actions, and he illustrates this phenomenon with interview excerpts from studies with children, adolescents, and adults. As a result, Day argues, moral actions are a function of the audience to which they are played, just as moral stories are a function of the audience to which they are told.

In the third chapter, Lyn Mikel Brown and Carol Gilligan focus on methodological considerations in the study of narrative and moral development from the standpoint of a relational psychology. Their method of interpreting narratives of relational and moral conflict—what they call their "Guide to Listening" to the ways in which people describe their lived experiences, focusing specifically on how they talk about themselves and their relationships—provides a way of entering relationships with other people, a way of listening to their narrative voices, and a way of attending to two relational or moral voices: the voices of care and justice. Brown and Gilligan highlight the literary, clinical, and feminist dimensions of this method and illustrate how it illuminates a phenomenon central to their research—the struggles faced by adolescent girls coming of age in American culture at this time.

Martin J. Packer, in the fourth chapter, provides a critical perspective on narrative approaches to moral development by arguing that while a focus on narrative as *representation* enables us to see how individuals understand and make meaning of their actions in the world, a focus on narrative as *action* is necessary if we are to grasp what really happens in individuals' everyday moral lives. He explores the links between narrative and action, arguing that when practice breaks down, narrative enables us to uncover new courses of action; hence action and narrative are linked internally and dialectically. Moreover, drawing on the work of Heidegger, Habermas, and Gadamer, Packer suggests that an interpretive analysis of action enables us to rethink traditionally problematic issues in the study of moral development, including questions about the ends of development.

Mark Freeman, in the concluding chapter, also takes up the problem of the ends of development. He argues that narrative and moral development are inexorably linked, not only because narrative provides a methodological approach to the study of moral development but also because both narrative and "the moral" (or "the good") are intrinsic to the concept of development as a progressive movement toward desired ends. He proposes that the self is constituted in narrative, that development can be seen as an effort at rewriting one's account of the world (and of oneself) by establishing a new interpretive context, and that morality is a sense of the good (for both self and others) established only, if at all, through debate and dialogue.

The purpose of this volume is thus to explore these emerging new directions in theory and research, to provide those interested in the study of moral development with an introduction to alternative approaches available for theoretical and empirical work in this rapidly changing field, and to stimulate further dialogue, discussion, and debate with respect to narrative approaches to moral development.

Mark B. Tappan
Martin J. Packer
Editors

References

Kohlberg, L. "Stage and Sequence: The Cognitive-Developmental Approach to Socialization." In D. Goslin (ed.), *Handbook of Socialization Theory and Research*. Skokie, Ill.: Rand McNally, 1969.

Kohlberg, L. *Essays on Moral Development*. Vol. 1: *The Philosophy of Moral Development*. New York: Harper & Row, 1981.

Kohlberg, L. *Essays on Moral Development*. Vol. 2: *The Psychology of Moral Development*. New York: Harper & Row, 1984.

MacIntyre, A. *After Virtue: A Study in Moral Theory*. South Bend, Ind.: University of Notre Dame Press, 1981.

White, H. "The Value of Narrativity in the Representation of Reality." In W. Mitchell (ed.), *On Narrative*. Chicago: University of Chicago Press, 1981.

Mark B. Tappan is assistant professor and co-chair of the education department at Colby College, Waterville, Maine. His research interests include adolescent moral development, moral education, hermeneutic/interpretive methods, and adolescent-adult social relationships.

Martin J. Packer is assistant professor in the School of Education at the University of Michigan, Ann Arbor. His research interests include social development in peer relations, hermeneutic methods, and the phenomenology of everyday life.

*When an individual "authors" a moral story in the context of a
dialogic relationship with another, she claims authority and
responsibility for her moral thoughts, feelings, and actions.*

Narrative, Authorship, and the Development of Moral Authority

Mark B. Tappan

> Responsibility for the world takes the form of authority. . . .
> Wherever true authority exist[s] it [is] joined with responsibility
> for the course of things in the world.
> —Hannah Arendt (1968, pp. 189–190)

As this chapter begins I invite you not only to ponder Arendt's reflections on
authority and responsibility but also to consider the following story of moral
conflict and choice told by Irene (pseudonym), a seventeen-year-old attending an all-girls school in Cleveland, Ohio:

IRENE: I've been thinking about this whole college conflict and choosing a
    college . . . because my parents wanted me to go one place and I didn't,
    and I had to either make the decision for myself or make it for my parents.
    And I visited the college that they wanted me to go to, but I didn't like it
    and it was hard to tell them I didn't like it. And I think I told my parents
    that, I mean, I could have gone there but I would have been doing it for
    my parents, and I think I ought to go to a school because it is where I want
    to go and not where my parents want me to go.
INTERVIEWER: What was the conflict for you?
IRENE: It was like whether or not to do this for my parents, because they have

---

Preparation of this chapter was supported by grants from the Cleveland Foundation,
the George Gund Foundation, the Lilly Endowment, and the Spencer Foundation.
In this chapter I alternate my use of gender-specific pronouns.

done, I mean, they have put me through school and bought my clothes and everything in life, raised me and I had the feeling I could have done it for them, because I owed it to them, but I also felt that I owed it to myself to become myself and do what I wanted to do, regardless of what they thought. I mean they are happy now with my college choice, and I am happier now that I made the choice for myself.

INTERVIEWER: Do you think you did the right thing?

IRENE: Uh huh.

INTERVIEWER: Can you say why?

IRENE: Because I felt good about it and I wasn't hurting anyone because my parents were disappointed but they didn't feel it was a big ordeal. I did it for myself and I felt good.

INTERVIEWER: Do you think you learned anything from this situation?

IRENE: I think I learned that sometimes I have to do some things for myself and not for my parents or for anybody else involved, because if it is something I have to live with then I think it is more important . . . sometimes you just have to think for yourself.

How do individuals, like Irene, come to claim authority and assume responsibility for their moral thoughts, feelings, and actions? That is, when faced with a dilemma that requires what she perceives to be a moral decision—when faced with the question, "What is the 'right' thing to do in this situation?"—what enables Irene to *authorize* her thoughts, feelings, and actions in response to that situation? These are questions about the emergence and manifestation of *moral authority,* the attainment of which, I claim here, is a central aspect of human moral development.

Any developmental theory is necessarily defined by its endpoint, its telos, toward which progress is assumed to proceed over the course of the life span (see Kaplan, 1983, 1986; Freeman, this volume). In the field of moral development theory and research, a telos has traditionally taken the form of *moral autonomy,* as articulated by the influential and widely known cognitive-developmental theories of Jean Piaget (1965) and Lawrence Kohlberg (1981, 1984), both of which are grounded in the moral philosophy of Immanuel Kant (1948). Moral autonomy, from this view, entails acting according to moral rules, laws, and principles that an individual independently constructs (or "self-legislates") for himself, not according to external rules or laws or to the determinations of nature (see Tappan, Kohlberg, Schrader, and Higgins, 1987). This view of moral autonomy has been challenged, however, by those who argue that because it assumes a "transcendental" epistemic and moral subject, it does not sufficiently acknowledge the degree to which human beings are always embedded in a particular relational, communal, and socio-cultural-historical context (see Benhabib, 1987; Blum, 1987; Gilligan, 1982; Sandel, 1982). One of my aims in this chapter, therefore, is to argue for a different developmental telos—moral authority—that defines an alternative approach to the study of moral development.

What does it mean to claim authority for one's moral thoughts, feelings, and actions? To claim such authority means, for one thing, to clearly express and acknowledge one's own moral perspective. It also means to honor, and thus authorize, what one thinks, feels, and does in response to a moral problem or dilemma, even in the face of conflict and disagreement. And, it means to assume *responsibility* and *accountability* for one's moral actions, and for acting on behalf of one's moral perspective. (See Niebuhr, 1978; Blasi [1984, 1985] argues similarly that moral responsibility is tied directly to an individual's sense of his or her moral *identity* and *authenticity*.)

Why is moral authority valuable and important? Evidence from social psychological research on bystander intervention (Darley and Latane, 1968) and obedience to authority (Milgram, 1974) suggests that individuals who experience little or no authority or responsibility in crisis situations are much more likely to act in ways that are harmful to their fellow human beings than are individuals who claim authority and assume responsibility for their actions. Moreover, a recent study of individuals who rescued or helped Jews during the Nazi occupation of Europe suggests that rescuers were not only more oriented toward developing and sustaining attachments to others, and more empathic, than were nonrescuers, but they also exhibited a stronger sense of "personal efficacy" (feelings that they could affect events and were responsible for doing so) (Oliner and Oliner, 1988). Thus, there is compelling evidence from a number of different sources to suggest that claiming authority and assuming responsibility for one's thoughts, feelings, and actions in the world enable one to act in ways that are helpful, rather than harmful, to others.

It is important to acknowledge the cultural specificity of the way in which I use the terms *authority, responsibility, helpful,* and *harmful* in this chapter. I am speaking from within a Western, (post)modern, postindustrial, sociocultural context where such terms have conventionally constituted and shared meanings; they may not mean the same things, or carry the same moral significance, in other sociocultural contexts. Moreover, it is important to acknowledge that my understanding of authority necessarily emerges from my privileged position as a white male living in a patriarchal culture. However, the notion of moral authority used in this chapter—tied as it is to a speaking, self-authorized, and, therefore, "resisting" self—holds the potential to provide a telos that is applicable to moral development across a variety of gender, racial, class, and cultural differences within our society (see Brown, in press *a*, in press *b*; Brown and Gilligan, this volume; Jones, 1988).

In this chapter I explore the links between the development of moral authority and responsibility and the ways in which individuals "author" stories or narratives about their lived moral experiences in the world. The action of authoring entails more than simply recounting a series of events in a temporal sequence; it involves telling a story, constructing a narrative, "narrativizing" (White, 1981). As such, it also entails *moralizing*: imbuing a story with moral value, thereby asserting or claiming authority on behalf of the author's moral perspective. Consequently, when an individual—a child, an adolescent, or an adult—authors the moral story (or stories) that she tells in the context of a dialogical relationship with another (her audience), she claims authority and responsibility for the moral thoughts, feelings, and actions that constitute the psychological dimensions of her moral experience (Tappan and Brown, 1989; also Tappan, 1990).

I begin with a discussion of the intrinsic connection between narrative and human experience in order to suggest that human moral experience, in particular, has a fundamentally narrative form and character. Then, informed by the work of Mikhail Bakhtin (1981, 1986, 1990), a Russian literary theorist and philosopher, I turn to a consideration of the ways in which individuals author the moral stories they live and tell, thereby attaining "authorship" and claiming authority and responsibility for their moral thoughts, feelings, and actions. I then outline Bakhtin's views on the process of *ideological becoming* (his term for the process of moral development), focusing specifically on the development of moral authority. Finally, I highlight the links between narrative, authorship, and the development of moral authority by offering some preliminary suggestions regarding how those who teach children and adolescents might encourage them to attain authorship, authority, and responsibility.

Narrative and Moral Experience

Let me begin by making two central points about the relationship between narrative and moral experience. First, when individuals make moral choices and decisions in their lives, they represent those choices and decisions, and endow them with meaning, primarily by telling stories about them. Human experience occurs inexorably in *time* and in *relationship,* the fundamental dimensions of narrative (see Alter, 1981; Gilligan, Brown, and Rogers, 1990; Heidegger, 1962; Ricoeur, 1981). Whenever it is necessary to report "the way it really happened," therefore, the natural impulse is to tell a story, to compose a narrative that recounts the actions and events of interest in some kind of temporal sequence. Such a story, however, does more than outline a series of incidents; it also places those incidents in a particular narrative context, thereby giving meaning to the human experience of temporality and personal action (Polkinghorne, 1988). Narrative is thus an essential means by which human experience is represented and interpreted, whether it is as mundane as a trip to the grocery store or as momentous as a moral crisis that changes one's life forever (see also Sarbin, 1986).

The connection between narrative and the representation of specifically moral experiences provides the focus for my second point. I assume that one of the primary functions of narrative in culture is to endow a certain sequence of events with moral meaning; in making this assumption I follow White's (1981) analysis of what he calls "narrativity." White argues that what distinguishes a narrative of certain events from a simple listing of those events in a temporal sequence is that the narrative, by definition, stands in relation to a particular moral perspective, on behalf of which that narrative attempts to assert authority. A narrative, therefore, attempts to endow a sequence of events with the kind of legitimacy and meaning that would justify and sustain the moral perspective on behalf of which it is written or told: "If every fully realized story . . . is a kind of allegory, points to a moral, or endows events, whether real or imaginary, with a significance that they do not possess as a mere sequence, then it seems possible to conclude that every . . . narrative has as its latent or manifest purpose the desire to moralize the events of which it treats" (White, 1981, pp. 13–14).

Thus, according to White, the author of a narrative asserts his authority by telling a story about a particular series of events, thereby giving meaning to those events. In other words, an author, by imposing a narrative form and plot on a sequence of events, gives to those events the meaning, value, and formal coherence that only stories possess: "The demand for closure in the . . . story is a demand for moral meaning, a demand that sequences of events be assessed as to their significance as elements of a *moral* drama" (1981, p. 20; see also Burke, 1969). One can never narrativize, therefore, without, at the same time, moralizing.

This view of narrative can be taken one step further, however, to suggest not only that narrative plays an essential role in representing and giving meaning to human experience and action but also that human action has an intrinsic narrative structure in and of itself (see Packer, this volume, for an exploration of this argument). MacIntyre (1981, pp. 194, 197) claims that narrative is "the basic and essential genre for the characterization of human actions" because human actions are "enacted narratives" (see also Sarbin, 1986). Consequently, narrative helps us to understand and interpret human actions, both the actions of self and the actions of others:

> In successfully identifying and understanding what someone else is doing [or has done] we always move toward placing a particular episode in the context of a set of narrative histories, histories both of the individuals concerned and of the settings in which they act and suffer. It is now becoming clear that we render the actions of others intelligible in this way because action itself has a basically historical character. It is because we all live out narratives in our lives and because we understand our own lives in terms of the narratives that we live out that the form of narrative is appropriate for understanding the actions of others. Stories

are lived before they are told—except in the case of fiction [MacIntyre, 1981, p. 197].

It is important to acknowledge, however, that this perspective on the narrative character of human action and experience—particularly of moral action and experience—does not imply that individuals are free simply to live out, and thus to tell, any story that they choose. Rather, the view is premised on the fact that narratives play a central role in the culture in which an individual lives, that is, they function as "tools" to mediate human action, and thus to shape and organize human experience (see Bruner, 1986, 1990). In other words, each and every culture has a particular set of narratives and stories that are passed down from generation to generation, and this set provides narrative structures that both enable and constrain the thoughts, feelings, and actions of everyday experience. As MacIntyre (1981, p. 201) says, "I can only answer the question 'What am I to do?' if I can answer the prior question 'Of what story or stories do I find myself a part?' "

Another way to make this argument is to suggest that the narratives in a culture provide common discursive "forestructures" that not only guide and direct how individuals interpret and make sense of actions and experiences over time but also shape and organize those actions and experiences in the first place (Gergen and Gergen, 1986). This view points to the powerful link that exists between human experience and the ways in which humans symbolically represent such experience. In particular, it suggests that experience (and action) must be expressed and represented in signs, whether linguistic or nonlinguistic, if it is to have any meaning or significance in an individual's life (see Vološinov, 1986). In other words, human action has an inherently narrative/historical character and structure simply because cultural narratives and stories provide the symbolic means by which such actions must necessarily be engaged, expressed, and represented—and therefore experienced.

Authoring and Authorship

Such a view of narrative and human experience necessarily raises questions about authoring and authorship. Specifically, does it make sense to see individuals as the "authors" of the moral stories that they live and tell? Is it helpful, in other words, to use such terms, traditionally associated with works of literature, in an analysis of the narrative character of human moral experience? I answer in the affirmative, for several reasons.

First, just as the author of a novel is, in a fundamental sense, the originator, the creator, the constructor of the story that she tells, so too does the individual function, in the same way, as the originator, the creator, the constructor of her life story, and of the thoughts, feelings, and actions therein.

This is an argument made with particular clarity by Bakhtin (1981, 1986, 1990). The activity of authoring is a central component of his analysis of human existence and experience (Clark and Holquist, 1984; Holquist, 1990). Bakhtin argues that meaning, in general, and values, in particular, are expressed in dynamic form through the activity of authoring. All of us who make utterances, therefore, whether they are spoken or written, are authors: "We operate out of a point of view and shape values into forms" (Clark and Holquist, 1984, p. 10). Moreover, how we author our lives—how we articulate and construct who we are—shapes that we think, how we feel, and what we do. In addition, because Bakhtin treats morality and values not in the context of an abstract philosophical system but rather as the "practical work of building" (what he calls "architectonics"), he highlights the fact that "by shaping answers in the constant activity of our dialogue with the world, we enact the architectonics of our own responsibility" (Clark and Holquist, 1984, p. 10).

Bakhtin thus points to a second reason why it is helpful to use the notions of authoring and authorship in an analysis of human action and experience. Not only is an author the originator and creator of his story, he is also responsible and accountable for it. As such, as authors of our own lives, we are necessarily responsible and accountable for our thoughts, feelings, and actions in the world: "Human beings can be held to account for that of which they are the authors" (MacIntyre, 1981, p. 195). In other words, as authors we must assume authority for our lives, because, as Arendt (1968) suggests, authority is always inexorably connected to responsibility (see also Hanson, 1986).

Bakhtin (1990), therefore, sees a crucial link between authorship, responsibility (or what he calls "answerability"), and authority; it arises from his view of life as action, movement, energy, and, ultimately, performance: "Life as event presumes selves that are performers. To be successful, the relation between me and the other must be shaped into a coherent performance, and thus the architectonic activity of authorship, which is the building of a text, parallels the activity of human existence, which is the building of a self" (Clark and Holquist, 1984, p. 64). What differentiates human beings from other living creatures, then, is the potential for authorship: "The means by which a specific ratio of self-to-other responsibility is achieved in any given action—a deed being understood as an answer—comes about as the result of efforts by the self to shape meaning out of the encounter between them. What self is answerable to is the social environment; what self is answerable for is the authorship of its responses" (pp. 67–68).

Following Bakhtin, I argue that such authorship is clearly expressed in the stories individuals live, and then tell, about their own experience, particularly their own moral experience. For Bakhtin, the analogy between literary authorship and his view of "life as authoring" (Kozulin, 1988) represents an attempt to use the paradigmatic case of the creation of literary texts to explore how the relations between self and other are crafted, both in art and in life. By this view, therefore, just as an author of a novel expresses her authorship, thereby asserting her moral authority, in the process of creating and writing her narrative, so do we, as individual moral agents, express our authorship, thereby asserting our own authority and responsibility, through the stories we live and tell: "Our ultimate act of authorship results in the text which we call ourself" (Holquist, 1986, p. 67).

It is important to note, however, that Bakhtin's analogy between literary authorship and life as authoring does not mean that either the novelist or the individual moral agent is free to autonomously or independently create, produce, or author a narrative that exists uniquely on its own. Rather, both the novelist and the individual moral agent are necessarily embedded in a particular sociocultural context, and a specific semiotic and linguistic milieu, out of which come voices, languages, and forms of discourse that serve to shape and mediate their psychological functioning and their experience (see Tappan, 1991; Wertsch, 1989, 1991).

Bakhtin (1981), like Vygotsky (1962, 1978), argues that the human psyche originates in the context of social relationships and social interaction, as interpsychological relations and processes are "internalized" to become intrapsychological relations and processes. The process that Bakhtin proposes to explain how this occurs hinges on the notion of *voice*. In brief, he suggests that the different voices that an individual hears growing up, composed of words, utterances, forms of discourse, and language are all internalized via the process of listening. These different voices are then represented and preserved in the psyche, where they engage in a constant *inner dialogue* with each other. Thus, we might imagine that a child growing up would have internalized the voices of his parents, his grandparents, his teachers, his friends, his favorite characters from T.V. and the movies, and even perhaps favorite characters from books that he reads. All of these voices would then exist in some kind of ongoing, dynamic, inner dialogue within his psyche—in dialogue, gradually, with his own emerging voice. (Day, this volume, captures this experience of inner dialogue between different voices, in his discussion of what he calls the "moral audience.")

The activity of authoring, therefore, always takes place in the context of a relationship, in the context of an ongoing dialogue between self and others. The utterances that an author produces, whether words or texts, or thoughts, feelings, and actions, thus do not arise ex nihilo from a single, solitary mind. Instead, such utterances emerge from a *dialogical relation* that must be the primary unit of analysis. As such, Bakhtin (who also published under the name of Vološinov) argues that the authorship of any text, whether it is a literary text or a text constituted by speech or utterance in everyday life, is necessarily shared between self and other:

> [The] word is a two-sided act. It is determined equally by *whose* word it
> is and *for whom* it is meant. As word, it is precisely *the product of the*

reciprocal relationship between speaker and listener, addresser and addressee. Each and every word expresses the "one" in relation to the "other." I give myself verbal shape from another's point of view, ultimately, from the point of view of the community to which I belong. A word is a bridge thrown between myself and another. If one end of the bridge depends on me, then the other depends on my addressee. A word is territory shared by both addresser and addressee, by the speaker and his interlocutor [Vološinov, 1986, p. 86; emphasis in original].

Does not such a dialogic conception of the activity of authoring, however, call into question the link between authorship and notions of authority, responsibility, and accountability? That is, if authorship is always shared, how is it possible to hold an individual author accountable or answerable for her actions? Must one, in other words, hold either a view of an individual autonomous self who is radically responsible for her own actions, and thus who authors her actions as an exercise of her own free will, or a view that an individual's actions are determined in some fundamental sense by the other with whom she is in relationship and dialogue?

To answer these questions, we must turn to Bakhtin's view of *dialogism*— a complex notion that, like all of his ideas, eschews simple, dichotomous, either/or distinctions. Individuals are, indeed, responsible, accountable, and answerable for their own actions, not because they are independent, autonomous agents acting on their own in the world, but rather because it is only through dialogues and relationships with others that the authority and responsibility of self can be constituted in the first place. In other words, Bakhtin's view of the self-other relationship does not emphasize the single, solitary self always in danger of succumbing to its own solipsistic subjectivity. Moreover, the self "is not a presence wherein is lodged the ultimate privilege of the real, the source of sovereign intention and guarantor of unified meaning" (Clark and Holquist, 1984, p. 65). Thus, the self is never whole in and of itself; it must exist dialogically, in relationship with others, if it is to exist at all.

As a result, Bakhtin articulates the dialectical (and somewhat paradoxical) position that the authority and responsibility of self and others are mutually interdependent: "As the world needs my alterity to give it meaning, I need the authority of others to define, or author, myself. The other is in the deepest sense my friend, because it is only from the other that I can get my self" (Clark and Holquist, 1984, p. 65). In other words, just as authorship is shared, so too is authority shared. When an individual claims authority and responsibility for his moral actions, that is, when he achieves authorship, he does not do so on his own, "standing alone." Rather, he does so in the context of an ongoing dialogical relation with others— specific others and generalized others—on whose authority he draws to define and author himself and his own thoughts, feelings, and actions.

The Development of Moral Authority

How does the ability to claim authority and responsibility for one's moral thoughts, feelings, and actions develop over the course of the life cycle? Bakhtin (1981) provides a very interesting answer to this question in the context of his essay "Discourse in the Novel," where he explores the role that language and forms of discourse play in human life by focusing on the paradigmatic case of the novelist, as she uses words and language to create a narrative. Of particular interest to Bakhtin in this effort is the process by which the words, voices, and language of *others* are expressed and represented by the *self*. This is obviously one of the primary tasks of the novelist, as she constructs and represents dialogue between different characters in the novel. By extension, therefore, this is also a crucial task for an individual person, as she lives and tells—as she authors—her life story and thus internalizes the words, voices, and language of others that shape and mediate her psychological (and moral) functioning (Tappan, 1991). In addition, it is as a result of this complicated process of internalization and representation that the individual is able to claim authority and responsibility for her own thoughts, feelings, and actions.

The starting point for Bakhtin's discussion of this process is his fundamental claim that authorship arises out of a dialogical relationship between self and others. Focusing on language and forms of discourse as fundamental to human existence and experience, he argues that the "living language" lies on the "borderline" of self and other, that "the word in language, is half someone else's" (Bakhtin, 1981, p. 293). If this is the case, how does one make the words and language of others one's own?

> It becomes "one's own" only when the speaker populates it with his own intention, his own accent, when he appropriates the word, adapting it to his own semantic and expressive intention. Prior to this moment of appropriation the word does not exist in a neutral and impersonal language (it is not, after all, out of a dictionary that a speaker gets his words!), but rather it exists in other people's mouths, in other people's contexts, serving other people's intentions: it is from there that one must take the word, and make it one's own. And not all words for just anyone submit easily to this appropriation, to this seizure and transformation into private property: many words stubbornly resist, others remain alien, sound foreign in the mouth of the one who appropriated them and who now speaks them; they cannot be assimilated into his context and fall out of it; it is as if they put themselves into quotation marks against the will of the speaker. Language is not a neutral medium that passes freely and easily into the private property of the speaker's intentions; it is populated—overpopulated—with the intentions of others. Expropriating it, forcing it to submit to one's own

intentions and accents, is a difficult and complicated process [1981, pp. 293–294].

To briefly illustrate this phenomenon of linguistic appropriation, I invite you to consider not only Irene's interview narrative, presented earlier, but also Amy's (pseudonym) interview narrative, presented in the Appendix to this chapter. Irene and Amy are classmates; they tell similar stories about choosing which college to attend, yet their narratives sound very different. If Bakhtin is correct, we should be able to hear and identify a number of different voices speaking in Amy's and Irene's interview texts. (Bakhtin refers to this phenomenon as "ventriloquation," whereby, in a specific utterance, one voice [or set of voices] speaks *through* another voice; see Wertsch, 1991.) The multiplicity of voices is most clear in Amy's text, where she explicitly represents her own voice and the voice(s) of her parents engaged in a constant dialogue in her psyche. She literally speaks in (or through) her parents' voice at times—for example, "They are going to be saying to themselves, 'We are paying for this, and she is going to be partying.' " The different voices speaking in Irene's text, in contrast, are less explicit. She represents the dialogue between herself and her parents more in her own words than does Amy. That is, she has integrated her parents' voice and her own more clearly than has Amy. Nevertheless, in Irene's statement "my parents were disappointed but they didn't feel it was a big ordeal," we can hear rather clearly the voice of her parents, telling her about their disappointment.

This kind of narrative analysis ultimately focuses, therefore, on the *speaking person* and his discourse, both in the novel and in real life. In order to understand and interpret the meaning of another's words, we have to ask (and answer) two interrelated questions: "*Who* precisely is speaking, and under *what* concrete circumstances?" (Bakhtin, 1981, p. 340; emphasis in original). Moreover, it is precisely by focusing his attention on the speaking human being in a narrative text that Bakhtin is able to explore the difficult and complicated developmental process by which the words of others gradually become the words of the self.

For Bakhtin this entails what he calls the process of "ideological becoming." A speaking person, according to Bakhtin (1981, p. 333), is always, to one degree or another, an "ideologue," because language is always "a particular way of viewing the world, one that strives for social significance." Therefore, an individual's moral perspective or orientation is a central aspect of her ideology—a perspective or orientation that is both shaped and represented by language (note that the word for "ideology" in Russian simply means an "idea system," without the political connotations that the word carries in English; Holquist and Emerson, 1981, p. 429). As a result, to understand the formation of an individual's moral perspective (and hence her moral development), particularly the degree to which she authors that perspective and thus claims authority and responsibility for it, we must consider the process by which she appropriates and uses others' words, forms of discourse, and language: "The ideological becoming [moral development] of a human being . . . is the process of selectively assimilating the words of others" (1981, p. 341).

This process of selectively assimilating others' words is key to the process of ideological becoming/moral development because words and forms of discourse shape and mediate the functioning of the psyche (see Tappan, 1991; also Vygotsky, 1962, 1978; Wertsch, 1985, 1989, 1991). In this case, however, another's discourse does not function simply as information, directions, rules, or models. Rather, it "determine[s] the very bases of our ideological interrelations with the world, the very basis of our behavior" (Bakhtin, 1981, p. 342). In his discussion of the process by which an individual internalizes and assimilates the words of others, Bakhtin distinguishes between two different types of discourse: *authoritative discourse* and *internally persuasive discourse*. The distinction between these two types of discourse or ways of speaking rests on the degree to which the individual claims authority and responsibility for what he says, and thus for what he does; it also parallels differences in the ways in which children are asked to learn texts in school: "When verbal disciplines are taught in school, two basic modes are recognized for the appropriation and transmission—simultaneously—of another's words . . . : 'reciting by heart' and 'retelling in one's own words' " (p. 341).

When another's words are "recited by heart" they function as authoritative discourse. Authoritative discourse demands that we acknowledge it, demands that we make it our own: "We encounter it with its authority already fused to it" (Bakhtin, 1981, p. 342). "It is not a free appropriation and assimilation of the word itself that authoritative discourse seeks to elicit from us," argues Bakhtin, "rather, it demands our unconditional allegiance" (p. 343). Authoritative discourse is distanced, it cannot be changed or altered, it cannot be doubted, and hence there can be no true dialogue, and no play with the context that frames it (Emerson, 1986). It has, in other words, complete and unquestioned authority:

> The authoritative word is located in a distanced zone, organically connected with a past that is felt to be hierarchically higher. It is, so to speak, the word of the fathers [of adults and of teachers, etc.]. Its authority was already *acknowledged* in the past. It is a *prior* discourse. It is therefore not a question of choosing it from among other possible discourses that are its equal. It is given (it sounds) in lofty spheres, not those of familiar contact. Its language is a special language. It can be profaned. It is akin to taboo, i.e., a name that must not be taken in vain [Bakhtin, 1981, p. 342; emphasis in original].

When another's words are "retold in one's own words," in contrast, they become internally persuasive. Internally persuasive discourse is much more open, flexible, and dynamic than is authoritative discourse. When another's words are internalized they become one's own, or as close to one's own as is ever possible. Thus, when an individual speaks in internally persuasive discourse, she becomes, essentially, the "originator" or the "author" of those words:

> Internally persuasive discourse—as opposed to one that is externally author-itative—is, as it is affirmed through assimilation, tightly interwoven with "one's own word." In the everyday rounds of our consciousness, the inter-nally persuasive word is half-ours and half-someone else's. Its creativity and productiveness consist precisely in the fact that such a word awakens new and independent words, that it organizes masses of our words from within, and does not remain in an isolated and static condition. It is not so much interpreted by us as it is further, that is, freely, developed, applied to new material, new conditions; it enters into interanimating relationships with new contexts. More than that, it enters into an intense interaction, a *struggle* with other internally persuasive discourses. Our ideological devel-opment is just such an intense struggle within us for hegemony among var-ious available verbal and ideological points of view, approaches, directions and values [Bakhtin, 1981, pp. 345-346].

Thus, what I have called claiming authority and responsibility for one's thoughts, feelings, and actions, and authorizing one's own moral perspective, means to speak (and act) in ways that are fundamentally internally persua-sive, not externally authoritative. Furthermore, this distinction provides a helpful guide to interpreting interview texts, for it is possible to distinguish between a text in which a speaker speaks primarily in authoritative discourse and one in which a speaker speaks primarily in internally persuasive dis-course. As a brief illustration of such an interpretation, we need only once again consider Irene's and Amy's interview narratives.

Irene speaks in a way that is more internally persuasive, whereas Amy speaks in a way that is more authoritative. Amy represents the speaking voices of her parents and the external authorities in her life, and she clearly says that her parents "know better than me." In addition, by speak-ing in (ventriloquating through) the dissenting voice of her parents ("We are paying for this and she is going to be partying"), Amy illustrates the lack of true dialogue that exists between herself and her parents, whose authority is fundamentally unquestioned. Irene, in contrast, clearly claims her own authority in making her college decision, and while she represents her parents' voice at times, their words are interwoven with her own words. As such, she ultimately speaks in her own words, in her own voice, and thus says, in a way that is clearly internally persuasive, "I think you have to make your own decisions; whether they are good decisions or bad decisions, I think you have to make them for yourself."

Finally, it is important to ask the question, how does someone, like Irene, develop the ability to speak in ways that are fundamentally internally persuasive? That is, how does she, or anyone, develop the ability to claim authority for her moral thoughts, feelings, and actions? This is essentially a question about the role that language and discourse play in the process of moral development, specifically, the development of moral authority and responsibility.

Bakhtin's answer to this question invokes the well-known developmental processes of differentiation and integration (see Werner and Kaplan, 1956), to illuminate his view that the attainment of moral authority necessarily occurs in a shared social context, mediated by many different words, voices, and forms of discourse. As such, moral development, for Bakhtin, entails the processes of gradually coming to authorize and claim authority for one's own voice, while remaining in constant dialogue with other voices: "Consciousness awakens to independent ideological life precisely in a world of alien discourses surrounding it, and from which it cannot initially separate itself; the process of distinguishing between one's own and another's discourse, between one's own and another's thought, is activated rather late in development. When thought begins to work in an independent, experimenting and discriminating way, what first occurs is a separation between internally persuasive discourse and authoritarian enforced discourse, along with a rejection of those congeries of discourses that do not matter to us, that do not touch us" (Bakhtin, 1981, p. 343).

The force that drives development, therefore, is clearly the experience of *dialogue*—both between and within persons. Sometimes the dialogue is pleasant and easy; other times it is very difficult, characterized by conflict and struggle: "The importance of struggling with another's discourse, its influence in the history of an individual's coming to ideological consciousness, is enormous. One's own discourse and one's own voice, although born of another or dynamically stimulated by another, will sooner or later begin to liberate themselves from the authority of the other's discourse. This problem is made more complex by the fact that a variety of alien voices enter into the struggle for influence within an individual's consciousness (just as they struggle with one another in surrounding social reality)" (Bakhtin, 1981, p. 348).

This is precisely the kind of struggle in which Amy is engaged as she tries to decide, in dialogue with her parents, what college she should attend. She has not, however, liberated herself from the authority of her parents' discourse. As a result, while at times she speaks in what sounds like her own voice ("I want to go to this college . . . I think to myself that I would be happier here"), in the end she defers to her parents' authority ("It seems like they know better than me"). We also have evidence that Irene has engaged in a similar struggle and dialogue with her parents regarding her college choice. In contrast to Amy, however, Irene seems to have come to a clear sense of her own authority ("sometimes you have to think for yourself"), and she speaks confidently and directly in her own voice ("I owed it to myself to become myself"). Consequently, from the standpoint of the perspective outlined here, Irene has a more fully developed sense of her own moral authority than has Amy.

In sum, then, Bakhtin's view of the process of moral development, and of the process by which moral authority and responsibility emerge out of dialogue in the form of internally persuasive discourse, provides a unique perspective on the development of moral authority, particularly in adolescence. It highlights the parallels that exist between the ways in which a novelist creates his narrative and constructs an ongoing dialogue between his characters, and the ways in which an individual lives and tells his own stories—particularly his moral stories—in his own voice, as a result of internalizing and struggling with the words of others. As such, Bakhtin points to the importance of considering the speaking person, the "author," as the central focus of any investigation of morality and moral development, because virtually all our categories of moral, ethical, and legal inquiry and evaluation refer, in one way or another, to the speaking person and his discourse: "conscience (the 'voice of conscience,' the 'inner word'), repentance (a free admission, a statement of wrongdoing by the person himself), truth and falsehood, being liable and not liable, the right to vote, and so on" (Bakhtin, 1981, p. 349). (This perspective, in suggesting a link between the speaking person and moral action, points to the degree to which speaking is, in fact, acting, particularly in the political arena; see Arendt, 1958, p. 26). The task of understanding how an individual comes to speak in what Bakhtin calls internally persuasive discourse, and thus to assume authority and responsibility for his moral thoughts, feelings, and actions in the world, must therefore be the primary focus of a narrative approach to moral development that lays claim to a sense of personal moral authority as its telos: "An independent, responsible, and active discourse is *the* fundamental indication of an ethical, legal, and political human being" (pp. 349–350).

Conclusion

Let me conclude by briefly summarizing what I see as the most important links between narrative, authorship, and the development of moral authority, and by offering some thoughts about the implications of these links for education—specifically, education designed to encourage children and adolescents to claim authority and responsibility for their moral thoughts, feelings, and actions. Authorship (and authority) not only expresses itself through narrative, it also develops through narrative. That is, when an individual (like

Irene) is enabled or encouraged to tell a story about her own real-life moral experience, two related things happen: First, because constructing a narrative necessarily entails moralizing, based on a particular moral perspective, telling a moral story requires that she authorize that perspective, hence telling a moral story also provides an opportunity for her authorship (and authority) to be expressed. Second, telling a moral story necessarily entails reflecting on the experience narrated, thereby encouraging her to learn more from her experience—by claiming more authority and assuming more responsibility for her thoughts, feelings, and actions—than would be possible if she were simply to list or describe the events in question. Consequently, authorship (and authority) is both expressed and developed through opportunities to tell one's own moral stories.

But the action of authoring one's own moral stories never occurs in isolation; it always occurs in a relational and sociocultural context, in constant dialogue with the words of others. The words of others are assimilated and internalized, and, over the course of the life span, gradually one's own voice emerges, to claim authority and responsibility for one's thoughts, feelings, and actions. To make this claim is to speak in ways that are internally persuasive, which is to tell one's story in one's own words, not externally authoritative, which is to tell one's story in the words of others. But, even when such authority and independence are achieved, they do not constitute an individualistic, isolated, "here-I-stand" autonomy. Rather, they must be understood in the context of dialogue and relationship—an authority and independence captured more clearly by the term *moral authority* than by the term *moral autonomy*.

Needless to say, the sense of personal moral authority described in this chapter has its own vulnerabilities—we need only consider the kind of moral authority that Adolph Hitler claimed for himself to see the potential risks of this kind of telos. While I cannot address this problem in any detail in this chapter, my argument is that the dialogical and relational conception of authority and responsibility explored here—in which authorship and authority are necessarily constructed in genuine dialogue between self and other and thus informed by both compassion and respect—provides a way to critique unilateral, totalitarian, and oppressive abuses of authority.

With respect to the educational implications of this narrative approach to moral development, I suggest that teachers and educators interested in encouraging the development of authorship should provide opportunities for students to tell their own moral stories, to speak in their own moral voices, and hence to authorize their own moral perspectives and experiences (Tappan and Brown, 1989). These opportunities allow students to express and enhance their own authority and responsibility through the process of authoring. By representing the cognitive, affective, and conative dimensions of their own moral experience through narrative, students are therefore encouraged to reflect on their own experiences from the standpoint of their own moral perspectives. This process leads not only to an increased sense of authority and authorization on behalf of that perspective but also to an increased sense of responsibility for action. Thus, teachers must listen carefully, respectfully, and responsively to such stories, thereby supporting and encouraging the emergence of each student's own authority and sense of self-authorization.

In addition, teachers can provide various opportunities for students to engage in dialogue and to struggle with the words and discourse of others. This kind of event can take the form of open and public debate, conflict, and disagreement, but it can also take the form of really *listening* and trying to understand what another is thinking, feeling, and saying. For, as Bakhtin (1981, p. 348) says, "One's own discourse, and one's own voice, although born of another or dynamically stimulated by another, will sooner or later begin to liberate themselves from the authority of the other's discourse." I also suggest that teachers interested in encouraging students to claim authority for their thoughts, feelings, and actions and to authorize their voices must be able to listen for and to interpret the different voices of authority that are present in students' texts, both spoken and written. The ability to identify these voices, and to distinguish between authoritative discourse and internally persuasive discourse, is the basis for teachers to support the gradual emergence of voice, authority, self-authorization, and responsibility in the context of internally persuasive discourse.

In the end, therefore, teachers and students must jointly assume authority and responsibility for the world, as it is in the present, and as it will be in the future. As Arendt (1968, p. 196) says, it is in our commitment to education that "we decide whether we love our children enough not to expel them from our world and leave them to their own devices, nor to strike from their hands their chance of undertaking something new, something unforeseen by us, but to prepare them in advance for the task of renewing a common world." As such, it is in the relationship between teachers and students, and in the ongoing dialogue between them, that authority and responsibility for themselves and the world must be forged.

APPENDIX: Amy's (Age Seventeen) Interview Narrative

AMY: Now I am going through the big decision of what college to go to and one school I applied to is big and it sounds like it would be so much fun because it's like a party school. And then the other one is little, it's an excellent school, but the social life is not as good. And one side of me is saying, "Go party, party, party," and the other side of me is saying, "No, your parents are paying all this money for you to get a good education," and my parents are pushing me towards the good education and I am fighting with them saying I want to have a little fun. And I know I am going to end up deciding what they want me to do because they are paying for it, and although they say it is my decision, it is like something inside of me saying, you know, "You have to please your parents and you have to do what your parents want you to do and your parents are paying all this money for you to get a good education, so you have to do what they want you to do." And I have been fighting with this for months trying to decide what to do and I still haven't come to a conclusion. I am a very bad decision-maker, and so I make the fewest decisions possible because one side of me says one thing and another side says another thing.

INTERVIEWER: So what would you say is the conflict for you in this situation?

AMY: The conflict is that I want to do one thing and my parents want me to do another thing, and if I say I want to go to this college, they will say, "Fine," but I know down inside they are going to be mad that I chose that college, and I know they are going to be saying to themselves, "We are paying for this and she is going to be partying." And I know down inside they won't be happy, and it's do I want to be happy or do I want to make them happy? And I mean, I'm sure I would be happy also because I am pretty much, I really don't have any problems fitting in wherever I go, but I also think to myself that I would be happier here, but then I think to myself, I would be happy wherever I go. So, should I just go along with what my parents want me to do? . . . I am always worried about pleasing my parents.

INTERVIEWER: Could you say a little more about that?

AMY: Well, I mean, I'll feel like I let my parents down, if they are there for me, I should always try and be there for them and do what they think is right. Because they have always, you know, helped me along and I am sure that, to me it seems like they know better than me. I know they talk with their friends about the different schools and they probably know better and it just gets to a point where why bother fighting because parents are probably right anyway?

References

Alter, R. *The Art of Biblical Narrative.* New York: Basic Books, 1981.

Arendt, H. *The Human Condition.* Chicago: University of Chicago Press, 1958.

Arendt, H. *Between Past and Future.* New York: Penguin Books, 1968.

Bakhtin, M. M. *The Dialogic Imagination.* (C. Emerson and M. Holquist, trans.) Austin: University of Texas Press, 1981.

Bakhtin, M. M. *Speech Genres and Other Late Essays.* (V. McGee, trans.) Austin: University of Texas Press, 1986.

Bakhtin, M. M. *Art and Answerability: Early Philosophical Essays.* (V. Liapunov, trans.) Austin: University of Texas Press, 1990.

Benhabib, S. "The Generalized and the Concrete Other: The Kohlberg-Gilligan Controversy and Feminist Theory." In S. Benhabib and D. Cornell (eds.), *Feminism as Critique.* Minneapolis: University of Minnesota Press, 1987.

Blasi, A. "Moral Identity: Its Role in Moral Functioning." In W. Kurtines and J.

Gewirtz (eds.), *Morality, Moral Behavior, and Moral Development.* New York: Wiley, 1984.

Blasi, A. "The Moral Personality: Reflections for Social Science and Education." In M. Berkowitz and F. Oser (eds.), *Moral Education: Theory and Application.* Hillsdale, N.J.: Erlbaum, 1985.

Blum, L. "Particularity and Responsiveness." In J. Kagan and S. Lamb (eds.), *The Emergence of Morality in Young Children.* Chicago: University of Chicago Press, 1987.

Brown, L. M. "A Problem of Vision: The Development of Voice and Relational Knowledge in Girls Ages 7 to 16." *Women's Studies Quarterly,* in press *a.*

Brown, L. M. "Telling a Girl's Life: Self-Authorization as a Form of Resistance." *Women and Therapy,* in press *b.*

Bruner, J. *Actual Minds, Possible Worlds.* Cambridge, Mass.: Harvard University Press, 1986.

Bruner, J. *Acts of Meaning.* Cambridge, Mass.: Harvard University Press, 1990.

Burke, K. *A Grammar of Motives.* Berkeley and Los Angeles: University of California Press, 1969.

Clark, K., and Holquist, M. *Mikhail Bakhtin.* Cambridge, Mass.: Harvard University Press, 1984.

Darley, J., and Latane, B. "Bystander Intervention in Emergencies: Diffusion of Responsibility." *Journal of Personality and Social Psychology,* 1968, *10,* 202–214.

Emerson, C. "The Outer Word and Inner Speech: Bakhtin, Vygotsky, and the Internalization of Language." In G. Morson (ed.), *Bakhtin: Essays and Dialogues on His Work.* Chicago: University of Chicago Press, 1986.

Gergen, K., and Gergen, M. "Narrative Form and the Construction of Psychological Science." In T. Sarbin (ed.), *Narrative Psychology: The Storied Nature of Human Conduct.* New York: Praeger, 1986.

Gilligan, C. *In a Different Voice: Psychological Theory and Women's Development.* Cambridge, Mass.: Harvard University Press, 1982.

Gilligan, C., Brown, L. M., and Rogers, A. "Psyche Embedded: A Place for Body, Relationships, and Culture in Personality Theory." In A. Rabin, R. Zucker, R. Emmons, and S. Frank (eds.), *Studying Persons and Lives.* New York: Springer, 1990.

Hanson, M. "Developmental Concepts of Voice in Case Studies of College Students: The Owned Voice and Authoring." Unpublished doctoral dissertation, Graduate School of Education, Harvard University, 1986.

Heidegger, M. *Being and Time.* (J. Macquarrie and E. Robinson, trans.) New York: Harper & Row, 1962. (Originally published 1927.)

Holquist, M. "Answering as Authoring: Mikhail Bakhtin's Trans-Linguistics." In G. Morson (ed.), *Bakhtin: Essays and Dialogues on His Work.* Chicago: University of Chicago Press, 1986.

Holquist, M. "Introduction: The Architectonics of Answerability." In M. M. Bakhtin, *Art and Answerability: Early Philosophical Essays.* Austin: University of Texas Press, 1990.

Holquist, M., and Emerson, C. "Glossary." In M. M. Bakhtin, *The Dialogic Imagination.* Austin: University of Texas Press, 1981.

Jones, K. "On Authority: Or, Why Women Are Not Entitled to Speak." In I. Diamond and L. Quinby (eds.), *Feminism and Foucault: Reflections on Resistance.* Boston: Northeastern University Press, 1988.

Kant, I. "Groundwork of the Metaphysics of Morals." In H. Paton (ed.), *The Moral Law.* London: Hutchinson, 1948. (Originally published 1785.)

Kaplan, B. "A Trio of Trials." In R. Lerner (ed.), *Developmental Psychology: Historical and Philosophical Perspectives.* Hillsdale, N.J.: Erlbaum, 1983.

Kaplan, B. "Value Presuppositions in Theories of Human Development." In L. Cirillo and S. Wapner (eds.), *Value Presuppositions in Theories of Human Development.* Hillsdale, N.J.: Erlbaum, 1986.

Kohlberg, L. *Essays on Moral Development.* Vol. 1: *The Philosophy of Moral Development.* New York: Harper & Row, 1981.

Kohlberg, L. *Essays on Moral Development.* Vol. 2: *The Psychology of Moral Development.* New York: Harper & Row, 1984.

Kozulin, A. "Life as Authoring: The Humanistic Tradition in Russian Psychology." Unpublished manuscript, Boston University, 1988.

MacIntyre, A. *After Virtue: A Study in Moral Theory.* South Bend, Ind.: University of Notre Dame Press, 1981.

Milgram, S. *Obedience to Authority.* New York: Harper & Row, 1974.

Niebuhr, H. R. *The Responsible Self.* New York: Harper & Row, 1978.

Oliner, S., and Oliner, P. *The Altruistic Personality: Rescuers of Jews in Nazi Europe.* New York: Free Press, 1988.

Piaget, J. *The Moral Judgment of the Child.* New York: Free Press, 1965. (Originally published 1932.)

Polkinghorne, D. *Narrative Knowing and the Human Sciences.* Albany: State University of New York Press, 1988.

Ricoeur, P. "The Narrative Function." In P. Ricoeur, *Hermeneutics and the Human Sciences.* (J. Thompson, trans.) Cambridge, England: Cambridge University Press, 1981.

Sandel, M. *Liberalism and the Limits of Justice.* Cambridge, England: Cambridge University Press, 1982.

Sarbin, T. "The Narrative as a Root Metaphor for Psychology." In T. Sarbin (ed.), *Narrative Psychology: The Storied Nature of Human Conduct.* New York: Praeger, 1986.

Tappan, M. B. "Hermeneutics and Moral Development: Interpreting Narrative Representations of Moral Experience." *Developmental Review,* 1990, *10,* 239–265.

Tappan, M. B. "Texts and Contexts: Language, Culture, and the Development of Moral Functioning." In L. T. Winegar and J. Valsiner (eds.), *Children's Development Within Social Contexts: Metatheoretical, Theoretical, and Methodological Issues.* Hillsdale, N.J.: Erlbaum, 1991.

Tappan, M. B., and Brown, L. M. "Stories Told and Lessons Learned: Toward a Narrative Approach to Moral Development and Moral Education." *Harvard Educational Review,* 1989, *59,* 182–205.

Tappan, M. B., Kohlberg, L., Schrader, D., and Higgins, A. "Heteronomy and Autonomy in Moral Development: Two Types of Moral Judgments." In A. Colby and L. Kohlberg (eds.), *The Measurement of Moral Judgment.* Vol. 1. New York: Cambridge University Press, 1987.

Vološinov, V. N. *Marxism and the Philosophy of Language.* (L. Matejka and I. Titunik, trans.) Cambridge, Mass.: Harvard University Press, 1986. (Originally published 1929.)

Vygotsky, L. *Thought and Language.* (E. Hanfmann and G. Vakar, eds. and trans.) Cambridge, Mass.: MIT Press, 1962. (Originally published 1934.)

Vygotsky, L. *Mind in Society: The Development of Higher Psychological Processes.* (M. Cole, V. John-Steiner, S. Scribner, and E. Souberman, eds.) Cambridge, Mass.: Harvard University Press, 1978.

Werner, H., and Kaplan, B. "The Developmental Approach to Cognition: Its Relevance to the Psychological Interpretation of Anthropological and Ethnolinguistic Data." *American Anthropologist,* 1956, *58,* 866–880.

Wertsch, J. V. *Vygotsky and the Social Formation of Mind.* Cambridge, Mass.: Harvard University Press, 1985.

Wertsch, J. V. "A Sociocultural Approach to Mind." In W. Damon (ed.), *Child Development Today and Tomorrow*. San Francisco: Jossey-Bass, 1989.

Wertsch, J. V. *Voices of the Mind: A Sociocultural Approach to Mediated Action*. Cambridge, Mass.: Harvard University Press, 1991.

White, H. "The Value of Narrativity in the Representation of Reality." In W. Mitchell (ed.), *On Narrative*. Chicago: University of Chicago Press, 1981.

Mark B. Tappan is assistant professor and co-chair of the education department at Colby College, Waterville, Maine. His research interests include adolescent moral development, moral education, hermeneutic/interpretive methods, and adolescent-adult social relationships.

Because the moral life is distinctly storied and, in a related way, theatrical in nature, the phenomenon of the moral audience provides a narrative link between moral judgment and moral action.

The Moral Audience: On the Narrative Mediation of Moral "Judgment" and Moral "Action"

James M. Day

In this chapter I propose that moral actions are a function of the audience to which they are played, just as moral stories are a function of the audience to which they are told. Thus, I suggest that moral "judgment" and moral "action"—two concepts central to the study of moral development—are mediated as much by the narrative structure in which they are rehearsed, reviewed, and redefined by the moral speaker and actor, as they are by moral reasoning, or by immediate circumstances of moral conduct such as emotion, group pressure, or relationships. By moral "judgment" I mean the conscious features of moral deliberation that persons draw upon in decisions about what is right or wrong to do when faced with moral dilemmas. Moral "action" is the conduct in which they engage when making their ways through those dilemmas. I have deliberately placed both "judgment" and "action" in quotation marks because of my sense that the narrative approach in which I am engaged, and the findings and interpretations that are part of it, necessitate a rethinking of both the utility of those terms and the ways in which they have been employed in the literature of moral psychology, particularly the body of work identifiable under the rubric of moral development.

I make this proposal in the light of research findings from several

I am grateful to the editors of this volume for their invitation to contribute a chapter. Portions of the research reported here were supported by Boston University, the University of California, Irvine, and the University of Pennsylvania.

studies, all of which have impressed upon me that when participants give accounts of their moral conduct, they do so through the medium of stories. These stories are more than parallels to or corollaries of the information with which they are associated. They are central features of the meaning that participants have made, crucial elements in the behavior that has been observed and reported, and determinants of the "reading" that can be done of behavioral "texts" and interpersonal encounters, and they are related to the authorial process to which the researcher-reporter necessarily becomes subject.

Drawing from the narratives told by children, adolescents, and young adults, I develop the argument here that the moral life is distinctly *storied* and, in a related way, *theatrical* in nature. Therein, I delineate the concept of the *moral audience* to describe something that many of the participants in these interviews discuss.

These participants balk at the notion of moral independence. For them, moral action always occurs in relationship to other persons, and their actions are always performed and interpreted in terms of an audience. For these individuals, then, consistency of moral action has much to do with the consistency of the audience to which such actions are played. Moral principles are developed and sustained, or changed, in relation to the parties who compose the audience, and moral actions are mentally rehearsed before them. Moral actions are then retrospectively analyzed and evaluated in terms of the same audience.

On the basis of my interpretation of these interview narratives, I argue that we can understand both moral judgment and moral action only when we can grasp the nature of the actor's relationship to the audience(s) before whom he or she most centrally acts. I also suggest that moral development must be understood in terms of the formation and transformation of moral audiences in the experience of moral actors. The questions of how such an audience comes to be central, how the forms and meanings of the audience change over time, in what ways its composition occurs, how and when there are substitutions in its membership, and how changes in conduct appear to be related to changes in the audience define, in part, the future direction for this narrative approach to the study of moral development.

The Moral Audience: Participants' Accounts

Several excerpts from participants' accounts of moral decision making are presented here. One of the participants is a former student that I knew when I was a graduate instructor at the University of Pennsylvania, two are from a group of interviewees who participated in an ongoing, longitudinal study of adult moral development (Connor, 1989; Connor and Day, forthcoming; Day, in press *a*, in press *b*, forthcoming *a*), and the fourth is from a series of interviews conducted at an early childhood center following the commission of a moral act by a young boy. Pseudonyms are used to protect the privacy of the participants. I comment briefly on each of the excerpts in the order that they are presented, before turning to a more thorough discussion of factors deriving from, and motivating, their inclusion in this chapter.

Porter. Porter, a young man of twenty-four with whom I conducted an interview, was asked to talk about a real moral dilemma that had occurred, or was occurring, in his life. At the time, Porter was an up-and-coming young account executive in a growing real estate development company. At the point that we enter his narrative, Porter has recalled a moral dilemma that has been particularly compelling for him:

PORTER: I was asked to represent the company on a major deal, really a big step for me. And I accepted the challenge gladly. I felt good that Nick asked me to take the account. He has really good business sense and this was a way of his endorsing my performance thus far. It was also an interesting case because of the development site, a great location in a suburb where people have a lot of pride in the appearance of the neighborhood, and a good challenge in part because of the size of the contract, in part because of the competition for it.

INTERVIEWER: The dilemma here was . . . ?

PORTER: That after appraising the account and going over the strategy for our proposal to the town, Nick told me to revise the strategy and to lie, to misrepresent what we would produce if granted the job; that in his view the account depended on my doing so and that of course my advancement in the company rode on the outcome. So for me there were several things, as I mentioned, involved. First of all, of course, I had to deal with the issue of whether or not to lie, but that was tied to other things—how to think of my relationship with my boss, Nick, given my reservations about his advice and at the same time the way in which he has invested in me and my growth at the company, how to deal with the town agents with whom I would continue to have a relationship on this or other accounts, what I would do if I didn't lie, lost the account, and lost my job (I have debts from graduate school, am solely self-supporting, have hardly any savings) as a result, all of those things.

I should add here that Nick is a really, is really different from me. Married, has a family, drives a big car, wouldn't live in the city, worked his way up and comes from a very different background. Very prejudiced in a way but works hard and has a sense for things that I need to learn. I think he looks upon me as someone he could have been or would like for his son to be like, he doesn't ask me directly about myself but is interested in any details I tell him. In a funny way I don't want to be like him, I don't want his life, but I don't want to disappoint him either, and I want what I can learn from working with him.

I'll give you an example of what I mean: Nick and I, just the two of us, were out in his car on the way back from a site that we had visited, this was another site on the Main Line, and we came through a neighborhood that was Jewish. We passed a Jewish day school and two temples, and Nick started making racist remarks, and then, really, it got ugly, throwing in comments about other minority groups, making a joke about faggots, and so on. It was really strange because in a way I knew that Nick was entrusting me with a kind of side of himself that he doesn't let other people see, giving me information about the world, while at the same time the content was totally repugnant to me. So formally I thought that I should say something, that it was inexcusable of me just to listen to that when I felt so differently and thought that giving the impression that I accepted his characterizations would be wrong, but on the other hand I thought that, well, he was entrusting me with this information, this view of the world and that maybe it was through this kind of thing that I could make the room, maybe later, to offer my own understanding of things to him. Maybe the closeness we would achieve would make that possible. And then he went on and starting giving really fatherly advice. He started telling me how the world works, how I should look out for this or that, how I was so talented and good but that I had better toughen up on some accounts and get a handle on the way the world really is. And this is what I meant, about the father-son thing; he's not the person I would adopt as my father but in a way he plays that kind of role to me in the business world, and for him it seems to be a little bit more than that.

INTERVIEWER: I wonder if you could tell me what you did and if you could trace with me the process by which you reasoned your way through the decision.

PORTER: I did make the presentation and didn't lie. I said exactly what we would do and why I thought it was best for the site involved. I told Nick about my decision after the presentation. My reasoning was that whatever the cost or gain involved, I couldn't live with myself if I would lie, that certain principles are more important than the issue of immediate self-interest and that lying would violate the sense of honor I have in upholding those principles, in participating in them. In the practical sense it also seemed to me that whatever might be gained from winning the presentation round would be lost if it were discovered later that I had lied, and that that would be worse for all concerned than to be, or have been up front from the beginning. You could say that I cared about the relationship I had with the client, and that I had become somewhat attached to the people in the community where the site was to be developed. I also didn't want to find myself in the position of having presented myself as one kind of person and then be thought of differently, either. That includes Nick, because I couldn't have won his respect from the start if it hadn't been for what I think of as being myself, and I think that I would have actually disappointed him by caving in to what he was demanding of me; he knew the thing was unethical and that I, I mean I really think he sees me as being an above-board kind of person.

INTERVIEWER: Is it fair to say then that the reasoning you've just described is what governed your action, your decision in this case?

PORTER: Actually no.

INTERVIEWER: No?

PORTER: No. What really clinched it was my grandfather.

INTERVIEWER: Your grandfather?

PORTER: Yes, he's deceased, but he was an extraordinarily important influence in my life, really the person to whom I looked for guidance. And, you know, I realize that this could sound strange, you're a psychologist and so on, but, well, I have these conversations with him. That is, my grandfather is still there in the moral sense, as a presence to whom I turn and with whom I interact when I'm going through the kind of situation that I'm trying to describe to you. Am I making sense?

INTERVIEWER: Yes, please, go on.

PORTER: Well, I have these moments, whenever I face a really big moral decision. I think of the people to whom I would explain myself, some from my family, some among my friends. I think of the account I would give of my actions, and of the way they would think of me. I actually picture the dilemma and picture the people in my head and walk through an explanation of what I'm doing in the situation to those people. . . . It's kind of like a rehearsal for the thing I will do both in the sense of doing the "action" [the quotation marks are Porter's] but also the way I will tell the story about what I've done once it has been done in the way I'm sort of rehearsing it. But it's my grandfather who is the bottom line. So in this case I thought of all that, thought of the story I would tell about what happened, and most of all thought of how I would explain a decision to lie or not to lie to my grandfather, and that was it, I mean I clearly couldn't lie and explain it with any satisfaction to him. I couldn't be me, the person I am or want to be to him, and do that, and I couldn't bear the disappointment he would feel toward me.

Porter's account is especially interesting because it demonstrates the complexity of moral decision making, lends itself to a variety of compelling and valid interpretations, and yet it illustrates the crucial role that narrative plays in the moral life of a reasoner who articulates with relative ease some already standard formulas of moral judgment-action relationships.

Blasi's (1984) emphasis on integrity and identity is clearly supported by Porter's account ("I couldn't lie and still be me"). Similarly, Rest's (1986) factors that qualify action as moral are present: assessment of the situation as a moral situation, the presence of a possible "right" solution that is known or intuited by the actor, the option to effect such a solution as selected by the actor, and an action that follows. Moreover, Porter's language can be characterized in terms of rights and responsibilities, justice and fairness (Kohlberg, 1984), and care lodged in relationships (Gilligan, 1982); and he describes a dilemma that has occurred in a real social situation involving highly important, immediate, and concrete relationships (Haan, 1978). Also, the developmental dimension of this dilemma is particularly evident (see Connor, 1989), given Porter's age and the attendant young adult issues of forming a career that is in accord with identity and with a life "dream" (Levinson, 1978).

Note, though, that Porter rebuffs an attempt to place his action in terms of one, or a combination, of these modes of explanation. He proceeds, instead, to take the interview further, into an explanation that cannot be subsumed to the reasoning that he has laid out in response to my request for such a tracing of it.

With the mention of his grandfather, Porter reintroduces the language of a paradigm he has tried to make room for before. "I should add," he says, a story about Nick, and about the kind of relationship that he and Nick had developed. Using the paradigm of family, then more particularly of father and son, to explain both the distance and the closeness between Nick and himself, Porter embarks on the explication of a narrative process of *moral discrimination* that is simultaneously affective and cognitive, analytical and relational, and that he outlines as a storied and theatrical examination of identity. It is in consultation, and in confrontation, with his grandfather, a figure before whom he acts, and to whom, through the medium of storied discussion, he is morally accountable, that Porter "clinches it"; it is this narrative process that is crucial in the mediation of Porter's judgment and action.

Indeed, it is questionable whether the language of "judgment" and "action," apart from the narrative process, would be of any utility here. The territories reserved for judgment and action are both reduced to unrelated separation and brought together as mutually determining processes in this account; without the inclusion of narrative, both in Porter's story of his relationship to Nick and in his account of how his decision was made, judgment and action are marooned from each other. With the inclusion of narrative, however, judgment and action are intimately related: Porter rehearses action in order to effect judgment, judges the rehearsal that he has made in order to account for himself before a judging and consulting grandfather, constructs a story with which he can live in the relationship that means the most to him as a moral actor, and acts in keeping with the storied reality in which he lives. Thus, even before the stories that one may imagine to have followed the actual presentation of a real estate development scheme (the stories that Porter may have told to the town planners, to Nick, to associates, friends, and family), the narrative ground has become a place where judgment and action have, in several ways, already met in order to produce a psychological house in which Porter can dwell.

Sandy and Kim. Sandy, a young executive in metropolitan Los Angeles, spoke with me about moral influences in her life (Day, in press *a*, forthcoming *b*). Referring to a recent dilemma that she had faced, she observed that several factors affected her moral choices, her follow-through, and her understanding of whether or not she had done the right thing. Sandy's account also suggests that there is an audience that figures in her own experience, and that its presence affects her understanding of her own development and of the independence that she deems important to address with me:

SANDY: I think that we're all accountable, in the end, to someone. You may become more independent as you go along and develop, in that sense, a wider pool of resources from which to draw. As you accumulate experience, there's more to consider and to work from, and in that way you're hopefully not quite so tied to the framework in which you started. But are you ever really independent? I don't know, or I should say that I don't think so. I think that there's always a sense in which you are explaining yourself to someone, always someone to whom you matter, whose understanding you seek, whose care you need in order to keep going.

INTERVIEWER: Someone to whom you appeal, in a way?

SANDY: Someone to whom you appeal, to whom, as I was saying before about the Sierra community, to whom you can tell your story, both to justify yourself and persuade yourself that you really are a good person, and to whom in doing that you make sense of your situation. In my case I know I'm always carrying these people—my family at first but now it's more my husband and my closest friends—around in my head. I don't just appeal to them once something has happened, but, in my mind, when I'm going through the stage of figuring out what to do. I think about how I'll explain things and how that would affect the way it would feel to me to be known by them.

Kim expressed something similar as she talked about who it was that influenced her actions, in the moments when she was making them. Her experience of moral formation in a Mexican-American, strongly Roman Catholic family was far different from those in the Protestant and Jewish upper-middle-class neighborhoods and family settings where, respectively, Porter and Sandy began. Many of Kim's recollections of moral influence thus stemmed from her early years in a neighborhood where violence and discrimination were commonplace. Like Porter and Sandy, however, she lays claim to a kind of moral experience for which I am trying to account in this chapter:

KIM: Well, no, the other people in the situation, I mean the immediate situation, their opinions didn't much matter to me. There will always be some people who approve of or criticize behavior. That doesn't mean, though, that I wasn't aware of how some people close to me would have thought of my actions. I think a lot about Roger in those kinds of moments. I want to do the kinds of things that I could share with him and of which he would approve.

Kim and Sandy, both articulate observers of the moral life, make clear in these passages that there are "someones," as well as "somethings," that influence moral behavior. In addition to the persons involved in the immediate contexts of the moral dilemmas they have recounted, there are other figures who loom very large, and from whom, psychologically, as actors, they are not "independent."

These figures, furthermore, inhabit the world of referents to which Kim and Sandy turn in their efforts to be good and exert an influence that both precedes and lingers long after the dilemmas at hand have been resolved. Their distance in time and space (Sandy is often away from her husband and friends; Roger, Kim's friend, is deceased) does not diminish, and may, in these cases, actually enhance, their impact. Their moral power, it would appear, lies in their capacity to know and understand the stories told to them by would-be moral actors, their ability to discern good intent from failed effort, the way in which they are "there" when they are called upon for support by the actors and serve as forces of virtue in the lives they lead or have lived. There is something about how they do, or have done, things that exerts a claim on the moral concerns and standards of the actors.

Unlike Porter's grandfather, the figures in Kim's and Sandy's audiences are contemporary in age (in Sandy's case there has been a shift in membership from family to husband and closest friends); like Porter's grandfather, one of the audience members is deceased, and, like him, both are persons (or presences) whose judgment and care can be counted on. These figures in the moral audience are sufficiently different from the participants that they can be relied on for perspective and for vantage points that help to establish clarity where the waters of appraisal (of past, present, or future actions) are muddied, but they are also closely enough bound to the participants' frames of action that the actors' narratives can be understood. They are not so identical to the participants, however, as to mimic or become lost in those narratives in terms of the interpretations that they offer. Actions are performed in the field of their careful watch and reconstructed with the aid of their interpretations.

It is in this light that Sandy doubts the norm of independence, and that Kim asserts her independence from the immediate sphere of action. For Sandy, independence is never fully achievable because of the persons to whom she, and, she suspects, the rest of us, are always accountable. For Kim, independence from the sway of those in the immediate domain of moral decision is afforded by the care and perspective she can count on from Roger. In both cases, there is no reasoning that stands independently of relationships, no principle that is not associated with a person in terms of whom it has been embodied, no cognitive judgment that is not subject, and parallel, to a narrative process of moral interpretation. Both Kim and Sandy rely on theatrical rehearsal and narrative processing in order to make sense of the moral life, and it is through these media that they confirm it.

One of the striking features of the accounts presented here is that they provide access to thought processes that portray the capacity for sophisticated moral reasoning and, at the same time, show that reasoners resort to, and routinely employ, other devices in order to make moral decisions. For Porter, Sandy, and Kim, morality is relational and, in being so, is necessarily storied; for all of them, morality has to do with being accountable, which leads inevitably to a kind of theatrical rehearsal of the conduct that will later be judged, if only in the mind of the actor, by someone else.

Michael. From the outset of this chapter, I have indicated my sense that moral psychology can be properly understood only when the moral audience is truly known. The cases I have considered thus far all suggest that certain features obtain across the figures in the audience groups that have been identified, but there are differences among them, as I have also noted. Sandy's case, for example, exhibits an occasion of change in the moral audience— new members (her husband and her friends) are added. The final case, below, suggests that the moral audience forms early, that it already has a fairly firm structure before the age of five, and that it is operational in a way that profoundly affects action in the young life of its reporter.

Michael is a boy whom I met when he was four-and-a-half years old, in the early childhood center where he spent half of each day. Michael spoke with me in the interview reported here after he had intervened on behalf of, and perhaps saved the life of, another boy, younger than himself. Michael had seen the other boy dash into the street beside the day-care center, chasing after a ball that had been accidentally kicked there, and had run after him, alerting a car that was coming at a high rate of speed around the bend, and thus out of sight of the other boy. The car screeched to a halt, Michael grasped the other boy and hauled him back to the curb. The scene had been observed by a couple of adults who came into the center to report the incident, by a teacher who had seen it from some distance away, and by several other children, who had come running to the teachers in the building to give their account of what had happened. I spoke with Michael about ten minutes after the event occurred. A portion of our exchange follows:

INTERVIEWER: Hi, Michael.

MICHAEL: Hi, James.

INTERVIEWER: You're getting a lot of attention just now.

MICHAEL: Lots of people are talking to me.

INTERVIEWER: I noticed that.

MICHAEL: About that thing in the street.

INTERVIEWER: What happened there, Michael?

MICHAEL: I ran into the street because I saw Kevin run out there after the kickball.

INTERVIEWER: That's what you did?

MICHAEL: I ran out there, too, because Kevin is smaller and there are cars.

INTERVIEWER: Cars, yes, the street can be dangerous.

MICHAEL: I know that. That's why I ran out there 'cause Kevin is smaller and can't run fast.

INTERVIEWER: What about you, you and the cars, did you think of that when you ran into the street?

MICHAEL: Yes, but not really.

INTERVIEWER: Not really?

MICHAEL: Not really because it was Kevin and I play with him.

INTERVIEWER: What do you mean? That you didn't really think about the cars because of Kevin? You could have been in danger from the cars couldn't you?

MICHAEL: Yes, but you're supposed to help people when they're in need.

INTERVIEWER: And that's what you did? How do you know that's what to do?

MICHAEL: 'Cause my mom . . .

INTERVIEWER: Your mom says so?

MICHAEL: She says you're supposed to help people when they're in need.

INTERVIEWER: What about the cars? What does your mom say about running into the street?

MICHAEL: She says you're not allowed to run into the street because it's dangerous.

INTERVIEWER: Who else gives you rules about what you should or shouldn't do?

MICHAEL: Grandma Miller.

INTERVIEWER: What does she say?

MICHAEL: The same as my mom.

INTERVIEWER: Oh.

MICHAEL: And the Incredible Hulk.

INTERVIEWER: The Incredible Hulk? The Incredible Hulk gives you rules about what you should or shouldn't do?

MICHAEL: Yep, he does. The Incredible Hulk gets very big when danger is near, and he can do things specially to help people. When someone's in need he goes to the rescue. Like on T.V. that time when the Hulk was trying to save that girl. He knew he had to do it, and there was that big brick wall that was going to fall on her and it could have fallen on him too, but he went anyway and rescued her and even though the wall fell he was running away and he was so strong from doing the right thing that he was okay.

INTERVIEWER: Okay, but how does he tell you what to do or not?

MICHAEL: I just ask him, like before I go to bed at night or when I have a problem, and he just tells me.

INTERVIEWER: You just ask him and he tells you, just like that?

MICHAEL: Yeah, don't you know what I mean? Like he's just there and when I ask him things he tells me what to do.

Michael's story is included here because I believe that some features of his moral audience can be deciphered from his report. Michael says that he has run into the street, despite the rule that one should not run there, to save a smaller boy from danger. He violates one rule in order to obey another one and in this sense demonstrates from his early vantage point how complex the task of following rules can be.

His mother is important to him. She and he have a close relationship of which both are proud, and Michael understandably takes a cue from his mother. She has told him that one does not run into the street, and that one helps another when the other is in need. Michael invokes the "voice" of his mother in this instance, and we can imagine that he has actually heard it many times, in his head, when confronted with choices about what is right or wrong, good or bad to do (see Tappan, 1991). Michael's grandmother is also part of the picture, part of his moral audience. She is, just as Michael attests, both close to him and consistent with his mother in the things she tells him to and not to do.

Michael also attends, however, to the voice of the Incredible Hulk, a television character whom he avidly follows. The Hulk, he claims, also follows rules, but when danger is near he grows in size in proportion to it, becoming equal to the challenge that he faces. My claim here is that the Hulk is more than a role model or television hero for Michael. He is, as Michael puts it, someone with whom he actually communicates, who advises and looks after him—he is also a member of Michael's moral audience. Whether or not the Hulk has appeared to Michael at the moment that he has decided to run into the street is not clear, but it is clear that he could have, and that Michael has consulted with the Hulk about other moral decisions. Thus, his mother, his grandmother, and the Hulk are figures in an audience for whom Michael performs, whose standards he seeks to uphold, and to whose judgments he submits the things that he has done. The Hulk is thus part of Michael's identity and performs a function of monitoring with Michael the things that he can and cannot do.

Discussion

Bruner's (1986) observation that we know much about the paradigmatic or logico-scientific mode of thought, but astonishingly little about its parallel, the narrative mode, is pertinent to current problems in moral psychology. With recent exceptions (for example, Day, 1991, in press a, forthcoming a, forthcoming b; Packer, 1989; Tappan, 1989, 1990; Tappan and Brown, 1989), there has been little explicit attention given to narrative as a significant mode for moral behavior.

My interpretations of the interviews presented in part here suggest that narrative functions in the moral life in at least four related ways. First, moral actors *rehearse* what they might do with the aid of stories, they consider possible courses of action in terms of the sense that can, or might, be made of those actions through the stories that will later be told about them.

Second, reporters of moral dilemmas employ stories to do their work; stories as much as factual accounts provide what the reporters need to communicate what has happened. Thus, reporters, when prodded, provide stories in order to elaborate on what they have said, especially if they feel that they have not been fully understood. Such accounts function to explain behavior to figures in the moral audience, and to others in the psychological worlds of the reporters.

Third, reporters on the moral life engage in narrative acts to *sort through* their own understandings of what might occur, what they might do, and what has happened. They do this before the figures in the audiences to whom their stories are tailored, before whom the stories are enacted, and to the interviewer whose attention they must sustain. Thus, they employ narrative, somewhat paradoxically, to communicate through what Iser (1978) calls "indeterminacy"; they induce their audience (and interviewer) to participate in both the production and the comprehension of what is intended in the act of speech. By so doing, reporters thus "recruit" (see Bruner, 1986, p. 25) possible meanings from the persons whose opinions matter to them and expand the repertoire of their own possible interpretations of the acts they may perform or already have performed. As such they reinvent both their moral identities and the "texts" of the situations in which the topical action occurs.

Fourth, moral actors, who are, as I have tried to show, also narrators and interpreters of narrated actions and situational "texts," compare and contrast the narrative structures that they invent with the standing narrative structures in the social worlds in which they live. Porter and Sandy both hesitate to tell their versions of moral experience in part because they know that their versions contrast with the standard narratives about development that are pervasive in their cultural contexts, including the moral psychology that they have read. Their stories of relationships, of storied decisions and interpretations, and of mutual determination in moral action are at odds with the overarching narrative of independence to which they compare their realities. The moral life is multistoried, multilayered, and carefully crafted and conveyed to make sense in relation to socially constituted conventions of understanding. I suggest here, in line with others (see, for example, Gergen and Gergen, 1986), that such conventions are themselves narratives upon which the status of verity has been conferred.

Implications for Developmental Psychology. One of the hallmarks of developmental psychology is that it seeks to understand continuity and discontinuity across the life span. The accounts reported here suggest, however, that while formal reasoning changes (Porter's analysis of his situation is vastly more complex and sophisticated than is Michael's) in ways well plotted by developmentalists (for example, Piaget, Kohlberg, and Perry), there is another mode, of both mediation and report, that has not been well described. How this mode develops remains open to question, but there is significant evidence that there is a continuity in its form that is as apparent as the recomposition, over time, of its contents; one continues to tell stories and to be accountable to someone; one continues to consult and to rehearse, to appeal and sort through, although the parties to whom one does so, what one makes of one's relationship to them, and the conventions in terms of which both are measured may change. Thus, what "develops" consists not only in the self-contained life of the mind of someone acting *on* the world and interacting *with* it, as the cognitive-developmentalists have held, but also in the changing composition and modes of discourse that obtain in the narrative framing of self in relation to others who both inhabit the self and exist outside of it. Interactions and relationships pertinent to the thought that guides, and results from, behavior in the world occur simultaneously both within the behaving self and between that self and others outside of that self. Further attention to the relationships among forms of thought and the narrative structures and processes rooted in the human relationships to which they pertain may thus enhance the prospect that developmental psychology can accurately portray the changes and continuities in human lives that are material to their conduct in them.

Moral "Judgment" and Moral "Action." Kohlberg's (1984) model of moral conduct has been dominant for some decades within developmental psychology and is particularly pertinent here. As Connor (1989, p. 179) has observed, Kohlberg's model is "deliberately—almost ideologically—restricted to showing the potential contribution to eventual moral action only of moral judgment stage and substage" defined in strictly cognitive terms. This restriction has been both the strength and the weakness of Kohlberg's paradigm for our understanding of moral behavior. Kohlberg's model is in a sense an elegant and "clean" model: There are cognitions and there are actions, and where the structure of cognition advances, more desirable action will follow. Action is a function of cognition, within a Piagetian dialectic of ever-advancing approximations of the way the world really is. Thus, cognition is not only more adequate but also more truthful; and since moral deeds are necessarily related to the truth, there is something necessarily better about moral action when it follows improvement in moral cognition.

There are by now many extant critiques of Kohlberg's model, and of its utility for understanding real-life moral behavior. Of the many studies that have tested factors hypothesized to correlate with, or to contradict, Kohlberg's assumptions about the relationship of moral cognition to moral action, some have vindicated Kohlberg's model, while others have led to plausible arguments against it (see, for example, Blasi, 1980; Connor, 1989; Connor and Day, forthcoming; Day, 1987, forthcoming a; Gilligan, 1982). My own work, including that presented here, suggests that where Kohlberg's model *appears* to hold, it does so in part because of factors that are not well accounted for in the model. Research has demonstrated, for example, that affect as well as cognition drive moral action, even when viewed from within the framework of studies that appear to confirm a strictly cognitive impetus for moral development (Day, 1987, forthcoming b), and that deontic choice— on which Kohlberg's judgment-action relationship hinges—follows only in some cases from decisions about which action is moral (Connor, 1989; Connor and Day, forthcoming; Day, in press a). In this chapter I have endeavored to demonstrate that those who *appear* at first glance to describe moral choice in terms of Kohlberg's justice equation, do so in parallel, and in much more complex form, in narrative terms. Kohlberg's model is pertinent to understanding the choices made, but it is not sufficient for doing so. Other major models of moral judgment and action are relevant too (I refer specifically to those of Blasi, Gilligan, Haan, and Rest; see also Connor, 1989; Day, in press a), but even together, I suggest, they fail to grasp fully what occurs in the judgment-action relationship because none of them explicitly accounts for the place of narrative in the moral arena.

The interviewees' accounts, and my interpretations of them, presented in this chapter make clear that the moral of the story *is* the point without which other models are lacking. The storied fabric of the moral life is so complex, the moral self so richly inhabited by other voices (see also Tappan, 1991, this volume), that only a model tempered by recognition of interdeterminacy—of voices, presences, other persons, dialogues, personal narratives, socially given narrative structures, and other social factors—will have adequate analytic and descriptive power. Recognition of the moral audience as one feature that guides the moral performances of some moral actors is one step toward the more adequate model that I and other authors in this volume seek.

References

Blasi, A. "Bridging Moral Cognition and Moral Action: A Critical Review of the Literature." *Psychological Bulletin*, 1980, *88*, 1–45.

Blasi, A. "Moral Identity: Its Role in Moral Functioning." In W. Kurtines and J. Gewirtz (eds.), *Morality, Moral Behavior, and Moral Development*. New York: Wiley, 1984.

Bruner, J. *Actual Minds, Possible Worlds*. Cambridge, Mass.: Harvard University Press, 1986.

Connor, D. *The Moral Behavior of Young Adults*. Ann Arbor, Mich.: University Microfilms, 1989.

Connor, D., and Day, J. M. "Compensation and Exchange: Being Moral in Time." In M. Commons, C. Armon, and F. Richards (eds.), *Adult Social and Cognitive Development: Adult Development*, Vol. 3, forthcoming.

Day, J. M. *Moral Development in Laboratory Learning Groups*. Ann Arbor, Mich.: University Microfilms, 1987.

Day, J. M. "Narrative, Psychology, and Moral Education." *American Psychologist*, 1991, *46*, 167–168.

Day, J. M. "Knowing the Good and Doing It: Moral Judgment and Action in Young Adult Narratives of Moral Choice." In D. Garz, F. Oser, and W. Althof (eds.), *Der Kontext der Moralisches Urteilen-Moralisches Handeln* (The context of moral judgment–moral difference). Frankfurt Am Main, Germany: Suhrkamp, in press *a*.

Day, J. M. "Role-Taking Revisited: Narrative as a Critical Adjunct to Cognitive-Developmental Interpretations of Measured and Reported Moral Growth." *Journal of Moral Education*, in press *b*.

Day, J. M. "Exceptional Sierrans: Stories of the Moral." In D. Connor, J. Day, K. Kaliel, R. Mosher, and J. Whiteley, *Character in Young Adulthood*, forthcoming *a*.

Day, J. M. "Moral Development: An Affective-Cognitive Model." In M. Commons, C. Armon, and F. Richards (eds.), *Adult Social and Cognitive Development: Adult Development*, Vol. 3, forthcoming *b*.

Gergen, K., and Gergen, M. "Narrative Form and the Construction of Psychological Science." In T. Sarbin (ed.), *Narrative Psychology: The Storied Nature of Human Conduct*. New York: Praeger, 1986.

Gilligan, C. *In a Different Voice: Psychological Theory and Women's Development*. Cambridge, Mass.: Harvard University Press, 1982.

Haan, N. "Two Moralities in Action Contexts: Relationships to Thought, Ego Regulation, and Development." *Journal of Personality and Social Psychology*, 1978, *36*, 286–305.

Iser, W. *The Act of Reading*. Baltimore, Md.: Johns Hopkins University Press, 1978.

Kohlberg, L. *Essays on Moral Development*. Vol. 2: *The Psychology of Moral Development*. New York: Harper & Row, 1984.

Levinson, D. *The Seasons of a Man's Life*. New York: Knopf, 1978.

Packer, M. J. "Tracing the Hermeneutic Circle: Articulating an Ontical Study of Moral Conflicts." In M. J. Packer and R. Addison (eds.), *Entering the Circle: Hermeneutic Investigation in Psychology*. Albany: State University of New York Press, 1989.

Rest, J. *Moral Development: Advances in Research and Theory*. New York: Praeger, 1986.

Tappan, M. B. "Stories Lived and Stories Told: The Narrative Structure of Late Adolescent Moral Development." *Human Development*, 1989, *32*, 300–315.

Tappan, M. B. "Hermeneutics and Moral Development: Interpreting Narrative Representations of Moral Experience." *Developmental Review*, 1990, *10*, 239–265.

Tappan, M. B. "Texts and Contexts: Language, Culture, and the Development of Moral Functioning." In L. T. Winegar and J. Valsiner (eds.), *Children's Development Within Social Contexts: Metatheoretical, Theoretical, and Methodological Issues*. Hillsdale, N.J.: Erlbaum, 1991.

Tappan, M. B., and Brown, L. M. "Stories Told and Lessons Learned: Toward a Narrative Approach to Moral Development and Moral Education." *Harvard Educational Review*, 1989, *59*, 182–205.

James M. Day is associate professor of education at Boston University, where he directs the European graduate programs in developmental studies and counseling psychology. His research interests include developmental aspects of small group processes and training for dispute resolution and the assessment of narrative reports in relation to other accounts and measures of developmental stage and change.

In a psychology understood as a relational practice, the process of listening to, interpreting, and speaking about the stories of others is a relational act; such a psychology demands a method that is responsive to different voices and sensitive to the way body, relationships, and culture affect the psyche.

Listening for Voice in Narratives of Relationship

Lyn Mikel Brown, Carol Gilligan

We begin with four questions about voice: Whose voice? In what body? Telling what story about relationships (from whose perspective and from what vantage point)? In what societal and cultural framework? When these four questions are asked of traditional approaches to the study of human development, they reveal the canonical voice of developmental psychology (the voice generally construed not as a voice but rather as the truth) to be oracular, seemingly objective, dispassionate, and disembodied. Yet, paradoxically, this "objective and disembodied" voice also presumes, at least implicitly, a male body, a story about relationships that is, at its center, a story about separation, and a society that men govern within the framework of Western civilization. By changing the voice, the body, the story about relationships (including one's perspective on the canonical story), and the societal and cultural framework, we are attempting to recast psychology as a practice of relationship (rather than a profession of the truth). As such, we are also asking what relationships are good in the sense of enabling and encouraging what we call psychological health or human development. In part, the success of this endeavor depends on answering the question "who are we?", and on recognizing that, as psychologists, we are in positions of authority and power: We are able to (*licensed* to) treat people,

Preparation of this chapter was supported by grants from the Lilly Endowment, the Cleveland Foundation, the George Gund Foundation, and the Spencer Foundation. An earlier version was presented at the symposium *Literary Theory as a Guide to Psychological Analysis* (M. Franklin, Chair), conducted at the annual meetings of the American Psychological Association, Boston, August 1990.

assess people, test people, and write about people in ways that affect their lives, their thoughts and feelings, and even their economic and social opportunities. Questions, therefore, about voice, authority, truth, and relationships, which may be academic within other disciplines, become, within the field of psychology, highly personal and highly political questions.

We have created a method and a way of working that make it possible, at least in a preliminary way, to engage and to explore these questions. In this chapter we describe our approach in some detail. Responsive to voice, this approach is also attuned to the body, to the particularities of relationships, and to societal and cultural context (see Brown and others, 1988; Brown, Debold, Tappan, and Gilligan, 1991; Brown, Tappan, Gilligan, Miller, and Argyris, 1989; Gilligan, Brown, and Rogers, 1990). Our voice-centered method thus provides a way for a psychologist to come into relationship with another person, a way of listening by taking in her or his voice. In creating a method that is responsive to different voices, and that is also a voiced method (that is, a method that includes the voice of the psychologist), we approach psychology as a relational practice and construe the process of listening to, taking in, interpreting, and speaking about the stories, the narratives, the words, and the silences of another person as a relational act. By voicing psychology—making clear who is speaking—we therefore shift from professions of truth to a practice of relationship. We also shift away from a monotonic language of structures and stages, toward a musical language (of voices, themes, keys, and so on) that highlights the polyphony of human discourse, a shift that does away with the notion of a no-voice voice and rejects the notion of "objectivity" in the sense of a voice or point of view that is disembodied, outside of relationship, place, and time (Gilligan, Brown, and Rogers, 1990; Rogers and Gilligan, 1988).

Our "Guide to Listening," concerned as it is with voice, is both a literary and a clinical method: responsive to the layered nature of the psyche, the harmonics of psychic life, the nonlinear, nontransparent orchestration of thoughts and feelings, the polyphonic nature of any utterance, and the symbolic nature not only of what is said but also of what is *not* said. And, as a relational approach, attentive to body, relationships, societal context, and cultural framework, it is also a feminist method—concerned particularly with acknowledging the pervasiveness of patriarchy/androcentricity in American culture at this time in history and its effects on girls and women as speakers, listeners, and readers. This process of voicing, as Kate Millett (1970, p. 58) says, "a system of power [so] thoroughly in command, it has scarcely [a] need to speak itself aloud," provides, we suggest, a way to move beneath prevailing conventions and understand how those not represented as full human beings within such a system exist and resist, how they create and sustain their humanity both above ground and underground. We are thus attempting, as Judith Fetterley (1978, p. xx) puts it, "to expose and question that complex of ideas and mythologies about women and men which exists in our society," and also "to see," as Adrienne Rich (1979b, p. 35) says, "the assumptions in which we are drenched." In pursuing these goals, we bring to the surface the "undercurrent" of female voices and visions, so often filtered through a patriarchal/androcentric culture. Thus, we claim an affinity with feminist literary critics, who have contributed to what Rich (1979b, p. 35) calls revision—"the act of looking back, of seeing with fresh eyes, of entering an old text from a new critical direction" (see also Schweickart, 1986).

We begin this chapter with a general overview of our method and the way that it enables relationship with another person by taking in her or his voice; by so doing we clarify the literary, clinical, and feminist dimensions of our method. Then we address three questions: Why use this method? What can it offer a listener interested in exploring psychic life? How can it help a developmental psychologist, clinician, or educator wanting to know about the clarity, confusion, encouragement, or discouragement of voice? Listening to the voice of Tanya (pseudonym), a girl in one of our studies, first at twelve years of age and then at thirteen, we draw attention to what we have come to see as a critical moment or crossroads in girls' development and show how voicing the canonical no-voice voice—that is, speaking what is tacit, embedding this voice in a body and in relational and societal context—paradoxically allows girls and women (and others who struggle to speak within the current patriarchal/androcentric framework) to be heard and at least partially understood.

A Guide to Listening

Our Guide to Listening calls for multiple encounters with another person: One "listens to" a person's story *four* different times, listening, in a sense, for different voices of self telling different narratives of relationship. We believe that listening in these four ways is necessary to take in a person's story and to hear its complex orchestration, its psychological and political structure. Each listening, in other words, amplifies a different voice. While we use the term *listening* to describe the encounter with another person, in our research, based on open-ended semiclinical interviews with children, adolescents, and adults, we actually combine the actions of listening to interview tapes and reading transcripts of these interviews. The work with transcriptions allows us literally to trace voice(s) through an interview *text*. We use colored pencils to highlight different voices and to document their orchestration. This way of listening/reading has, in turn, affected the way we interview—the way we engage another, the way we listen for self, for cultural messages and stereotypes, as well as for resistance to such messages.

Thus, listening first for one voice and then another, the listener appreciates the intricate structure of a person's experiences of self and relationships. Individual words and phrases (the stock and trade of traditional research practices and coding systems used to categorize thought, feeling, and action) are meaningless in and of themselves to explain the "living utterance" (Bakhtin, 1981, p. 276). The living language, like the living person, exists in a web of relationships, and a person's meaning can become clear only if these relationships are maintained. By acknowledging that people live in relationship, and that language always exists in a dialogical context, this method enables us to begin to trace and untangle the relationships that constitute psychic life, and to speak both about our relationship with another person and about our encounter with a story being told in a clinical or research setting, as well as in a larger societal and cultural context.

The first time through the narrative, the listener attends to the story itself. The listener's goal is to understand the story, the context, the drama (the who, what, when, where, and why of the narrative; see Burke, 1969). The listener, like a literary critic or a psychotherapist, pays attention to recurrent words or images, central metaphors, emotional resonances, contradictions, or inconsistencies in style, revisions and absences in the story, as well as shifts in narrative position—the use of first-, second-, or third-person voice. Such close attention to voice helps the listener locate the speaker in the narrative she tells. (We use female-marked pronouns to refer to both the narrator and the listener, for the sake of convenience and clarity. Our method, however, has been used by both women and men, listening to the voices of girls and boys, women and men.) In addition, this first way of attending asks the listener to reflect on herself as a person who is in the privileged position of interpreting the life events of another, and to consider the implications of this act. An awareness of the power to name and control meaning is critical. The listener is asked to attend to her initial thoughts and feelings about the narrator and the story. In what way does she identify with or distance herself from the narrator? In what way is she different or the same? Where is she confused or puzzled? Where is she certain? Is she pleased or upset by the story? And she is asked to consider how these thoughts and feelings may affect her understanding, her interpretation, her response.

The second time through the narrative, the listener listens for "self": the voice of the "I" speaking in the story, and also the "I" who appears as actor or protagonist in the story. In the process of attending to self, the listener becomes engaged with or involved with the speaker; as she listens to the way in which a person speaks about herself, she is likely to experience herself coming into a relationship, so that she begins to know the narrator on her own terms and to respond to what she is saying, emotionally as well as intellectually. Like Rich (1979a), who describes her own process of coming to know the work of Emily Dickinson, she encounters not simply a text but rather the "heart and mind" of another; "she comes into close contact with an interiority—a power, a creativity, a suffering, a vision—that is *not* identical with her own" (Schweickart, 1986, p. 52). As the narrator's words enter the listener's psyche, a process of connection begins between the narrator's thoughts and feelings and the listener's thoughts and feelings in response, so that the narrator affects the listener, who begins to learn from the narrator—about the narrator, about herself, and about the world they share in common, especially the world of relationships.

Once the listener allows the voice of another to enter her psyche, she can no longer claim a detached or "objective" position. She is affected by the narrator, whose words may lead her to think about a variety of things and to feel sad, or happy, or jealous, or angry, or bored, or frustrated, or comforted, or hopeful. But by allowing the narrator's words to enter her psyche, the listener gains the sense of an entry, an opening, a way into the story in the narrator's terms. Thus, relationship or connection, rather than blurring perspective or diminishing judgment, signifies an opening of self to other, creating a channel for information, an avenue to knowledge.

These first two ways of attending to another's voice are central to a *responsive* listener and are thus key to what we mean when we call this a "relational" method (Brown, Debold, Tappan, and Gilligan, 1991). They are designed to highlight the relationship between a listener's life history and context and those of the narrator as represented in the interview text. But heeding Schweickart's (1986, p. 50) critique of reader-response approaches to literary analysis, which make no claims to feminism and thus overlook "issues of race, class, and sex, and give no hint of the conflicts, sufferings, and passions that attend these realities," our responsive listener's guide is also a *resisting* listener's guide, that is, a feminist method. A resisting reader, Fetterley (1978, p. xxii) suggests, questions "the very posture of the apolitical"; such a reader gives "voice to a different reality and different vision . . . [brings] a different subjectivity to bear on the old 'universality' " and thus politicizes it.

Our "resisting listener," therefore, listens against the conventions of the dominant culture, a move that we have made explicit in the third and fourth ways of attending outlined by our Guide to Listening. These final two ways of listening focus on two recurring relational voices in narratives of relational conflict (Gilligan, 1982; Gilligan and Attanucci, 1988; Gilligan, Ward, and Taylor, 1988; Gilligan and Wiggins, 1987). These voices articulate two different wishes and concerns about relationships: wishes and concerns about loving and being loved, listening and being listened to, and responding and being responded to, on the one hand, and wishes and concerns about equality, reciprocity, and fairness between persons, on the other. These voices, in other words, speak about love (care) and about justice (equality/fairness). A resisting listener attempts to identify these two voices and to distinguish when these relational voices reflect societal conventions of female and male behavior, that is, when they are narrowed and distorted by gender stereotypes, or used to justify distancing, neglect, subordination or oppression, and when they represent relationships that are healthy, freeing, or, in today's vernacular, "empowering." The resisting listener identifies the vulnerabilities inherent to conventional notions of love and justice—the potential for self-sacrifice or self-silencing and the desire for purity and perfection in the case of the feminine ideal (the "good woman"), or, in the case of the masculine ideal (the "real man"), the potential for self-aggrandizement and the desire to control or dominate. In this way, a resisting listener attempts to extricate herself from a patriarchal/androcentric logic, to create a space for her struggle to redefine or "revision" both self and relationship.

Tanya

To illustrate the use of our Guide to Listening, we turn to Tanya, a twelve-year-old girl of Indian descent, the daughter of two doctors, a seventh grader in a private girls' school in the Midwest (see Brown and Gilligan, 1990). Using this method, what can a responsive, resisting listener say about Tanya's experience of herself and her relationships? Here, we listen to Tanya speaking about herself and her relationships at age twelve and then the way that she speaks a year later at age thirteen. The full text of Tanya's interview narrative at twelve years of age is in the Appendix to this chapter. (Our Guide to Listening also mandates the use of worksheets, which assure that the listener leaves a comprehensive trail of evidence for her interpretations. The worksheets for Tanya's narrative at twelve are reprinted in their entirety in Brown, Debold, Tappan, and Gilligan, 1991.)

Listening to Tanya's narrative of relational conflict a first time, we hear her, at twelve, tell a story in which she is willing to take on an intransigent camp guide, and risk getting yelled at, on behalf of her homesick cousin:

> When we were at camp [two years ago], I went to camp with my sister and my cousin, and he was really young. . . . He was, like, maybe seven, and he got really, really homesick. It was overnight. And he was, like, always crying at night and stuff. And we had this camp guide who was really tough, and I was kind of afraid of him. . . . And he said, "Nobody's allowed to use the phone." And so my cousin really wanted to call his parents. And it was kind of up to me to go ask the guy if he could. So, either, like, I got bawled out by this guy and asked, or I didn't do anything about it. And he was my cousin, so I had to help him. So I went, so I asked the guy if he could use the phone, and he started giving me this lecture about how there shouldn't be homesickness in this camp. And I said, "Sorry, but he's only seven." And he was really young, and so he finally got to use the phone. So he used the phone, and then we had a camp meeting, and, um, the guy started saying, "Any kid here who gets homesick shouldn't be here." And he didn't say my cousin's name, but he was, like, almost in tears.

Tanya's story is about her cousin's homesickness, the intransigence of a camp director, and her decision, despite her fear, to help her cousin call his parents. The conflict was, she says succinctly, "me saving myself or saving him." She decided to help her cousin because "nothing bad was going to happen to me"; the camp director might intimidate her and hurt her feelings, but he "can't beat me up or anything." She realized that "it was worth, like, letting [her cousin] talk to his parents. . . . My cousin was screaming, has nightmares. . . . He wasn't being able to have any fun and he paid for it. . . . He was like almost sick, you know. That's why I guess they call it homesick." The camp director, she thinks, "was really callous." Looking back, Tanya says that it is obvious that her decision was right, at least for her. "It might not be for you or somebody else, but it's helping out my cousin and that camp director, it's a rule, but people are more important than rules." Besides, she notes, the camp director was contradicting himself; they say, "We're here to help our kids, to make them have fun." Her cousin, she observes, "wasn't having fun, he was just contradicting the whole slogan."

Listening to this narrative of relational conflict, we note that Tanya states the problem on several levels: as a conflict between saving herself and saving her cousin, as a conflict between people and rules, and as a conflict between doing nothing and doing something in a situation where she sees the possibility of doing something to help. The relationships involved are Tanya's relationships with her cousin, with herself, with the camp director, and with her friends, as well as the cousin's relationship with his parents. A possible contradiction in the story is between Tanya's sense that the right thing was obvious and she did the right thing, and her experience of conflict.

As we take in Tanya's voice, we respond to Tanya's story, recording places of connection and disconnection between Tanya's experience and our own. As listeners, we ask ourselves what we know about Tanya from this story and what this might mean for our interpretation. Through this connection, we draw attention to the powerful act of one person, the listener, interpreting—"naming"—the experience of another who only speaks within a narrative about a conflict with which she lived. In Tanya's case, the listener recalls her own experiences of summer camp, and on the worksheets she writes about her memories of "how powerful the counselors were" and "the rules which seemed arbitrary and unfair." As a white, educationally advantaged woman from a working-class background, she also wonders "if the fact that [Tanya] is Indian has anything to do with her choice" or her sense of obligation to protect her young cousin, or "if Tanya's privilege give[s] her confidence in the system"—confidence that the listener herself did not have at that age. In this way the listener attends to what she knows about Tanya, and what she knows about herself, to raise questions about her interpretation of the story.

The second time through the story we record the way that Tanya speaks about herself, before we speak about her. Here is Tanya's story in first person:

> I went to camp. . . . I was kind of afraid of him . . . and I was really afraid of him. . . . It was kind of up to me. . . . Either, like, I got bawled out by this guy and asked, or I didn't do anything about it. . . . I had to help him. . . . So I went, so I asked. . . . I said, "Sorry, but he's only seven." . . . I said, "This guy can, he can intimidate me but he can't beat me up." . . . I'll realize . . . I have to do this. . . . I mean . . . I'm sure, I was sure. . . . He was my cousin, you know, and we've always been kind of close. . . . Either . . . I helped him out or I helped my, or I didn't, like that was for him, or I couldn't go for myself because I didn't want to be like . . . I was really afraid. . . . It was me saving myself or saving him. . . . I mean, nothing bad was going to happen to me. . . . So I realized . . . so I guess he did kind of realize . . . I mean I would never see that guy again. . . . But I lived . . . I lived with my cousin. . . . I would never see that guy again. . . . It's just like my feelings being hurt and I hate being yelled at. . . . I guess . . . I'm sure . . . the way I saw it . . . so I don't . . . I guess . . . I know . . . I was really surprised. . . . I felt really good but I felt really bad. . . . I did something for him. . . . And it's kind of like a victory. . . . I'm sure . . . I don't know what it was. . . . It's obvious that was right . . . it is for me. . . . I felt it. . . . I could have gotten out of it easily. . . . It wasn't my feeling . . . I wasn't feeling what he was feeling. . . . I did have a little empathy, but, you know, not that much. . . . I could have gotten out of it and said, "I'm not going up to that camp director." . . . I almost felt like he did in a way, so I did, I did go up, you know, because I felt miserable having him feel miserable.

Tanya's voice carries the sound of a candid, confident, psychologically astute and shrewd twelve-year-old, concerned about her cousin and also about herself, indignant at the camp director's lack of concern, sure of her perceptions and judgments, stubborn, determined, and capable of making intriguing observations: "Either you feel it, like all the way, or you just, like, recognize it" (referring to the difference between her response to her cousin's homesickness and that of her friends).

Attending to how she, as a subject, speaks about herself in this drama, we hear Tanya's fear of the camp director ("I was afraid of him," she says three separate times) and also her clarity about the situation she is in; her certainty that although the director, who is "a big bully and he can have anything the way he wants it," might yell at her, he cannot physically hurt her. Knowing this, Tanya speaks about what she sees and hears: She *sees* her cousin's obvious distress; she *hears* his crying and screaming at night. And, taking in the evidence of her senses, her experiences guide her understanding: "He was like almost sick, you know. That's why I guess they call it homesick." At the risk of being yelled at, and in the face of the camp director's admonishments, which are supported by the camp rules, she finally determines that "I have to do this."

Listening, a third time, for Tanya's sense of love and responsiveness, we hear her speak about her concern for her cousin:

> He was really young. He was like maybe seven, and he got really, really homesick. It was overnight. And he was, like, always crying at night and stuff. . . . And so my cousin really wanted to call his parents. . . . And he was my cousin, so I had to help him. . . . And I said, "Sorry, but he's only seven." . . . He was, like, almost in tears. . . . The right thing was to go because it was for my cousin's good, you know. And he wasn't going to die or anything but, you know, he's like afraid to go to camp now, because he's like nine now. And he's like, he doesn't want to go back. . . . This guy can, he can intimidate me, but he can't beat me up or any-thing. . . . I'll realize that that's just the way he is, but I have to do this . . . just help [my cousin] out. . . . The conflict was that, like, it was like, he was my cousin, you know, and we've always been kind of close. . . . It was me saving myself or saving him. . . . Nothing bad was going to happen to me. . . . He felt a lot better. . . . My cousin was scream-ing, has nightmares, and it was really bad, he was with all his friends. . . . My cousin lives seven minutes away from us, so I lived with my cousin, but I would never see that [camp director] again. . . . [What was at stake was] kind of like the ego, you know, it's like nothing phys-ically and nothing that anybody else would see. It's just like my feelings being hurt and I hate being yelled at. . . . But my cousin, he was like feeling really, really low . . . really bad. He was like almost sick. . . . It's like, either you feel it, like all the way, or you just, like, recognize it, you know? . . . It's helping out my cousin and that camp director, you know, it's a rule, but people are more important than rules. . . . He was just a little kid. . . . My cousin wasn't having fun. . . . He was, like, really close, but I wasn't feeling what he was feeling, so like I did have a little empathy but, you know, not that much. . . . He was, like, very miserable and I almost felt like he did in a way, so I did, I did go up, you know, because I felt miserable having him feel miserable.

Listening in this way, we hear Tanya speak of her relationship with her cousin—"we've always been kind of close"—and her feelings in response to his pain—"I did have a little empathy but, you know, not that much. . . . I almost felt like he did in a way." Tanya's attentiveness to the feelings of her cousin and her wish to respond to his need are tied in with her own feelings because her cousin's unhappiness affects her. But his feelings are not the same as her feelings, as she states clearly; he is not she. Implicitly resisting conventional notions of selflessness and self-sac-rifice associated with feminine ideals of love, Tanya's care voice draws the reader's attention, instead, to her knowledge of human relationships and psychological processes, knowledge that suggests close and careful obser-vations. And when the camp director does not acknowledge her cousin's distress, when he responds by giving her a lecture "about how there shouldn't be homesickness in this camp," we hear Tanya's resistance to his view when she points to the visible signs of her cousin's distress and replies, "Sorry, but he's only seven."

Listening, finally, for a sense of fairness and a wish for respect, we hear Tanya speak about the camp director and express her feelings about his power over her and her cousin:

> We had this camp guide who was really tough and I was kind of afraid of him . . . and I was really afraid of him. And he said, "Nobody's allowed to use the phone." And so my cousin really wanted to call his par-ents. . . . So either, like, I got bawled out by this guy and asked, or I didn't do anything about it. And he was my cousin, so I had to help him. . . . So I went, so I asked . . . and he started giving me this lecture about how there shouldn't be homesickness in this camp. And I said, "Sorry, but he's only seven." . . . We had a camp meeting . . . and, um, the guy started saying, "Any kid here who gets homesick shouldn't be here." . . . And the right thing was to go because it was for my cousin's good, you know. . . . Like, I said, "This guy can, he can intimidate me, but he can't beat me up or anything." And I, I'll realize that that's just the way he is, but I have to do this. . . . I hate being yelled at. . . . He wasn't being able to have any fun and he paid for it, so he had to do some-thing. . . . The way I saw it at that time was this guy is, like, a big bully and he can have anything the way he wants it. So . . . I guess it was kind of big, letting, giving in for him. . . . He goes on . . . his, like his reputa-tion, you know, see that was a rule and he couldn't break it, but he said, "Yes, *but*," and then he started giving us the lecture. . . . But I did some-thing for him, my cousin, and it's kind of like a victory, you know, it's like you won over this guy, so be happy. . . . It's a rule, but people are more important than rules. . . . They were saying, "Well, we're here to help our kids, to make them have fun," but my cousin wasn't having fun, he was just contradicting the whole slogan.

Tanya reasons empirically from experience as she notes the absurdity of a situation in which the camp directors say, "We're here to help our kids, to make them have fun," and the fact that her cousin "wasn't being able to have any fun and he paid for it." It was also oppressive for a camp director to place his concern with reputation over the misery of a seven-year-old, and to take advantage of the fact that the seven-year-old was under his direction while he "can have anything the way he wants it." Tanya presents a complicated understanding of rules as structures that maintain order in relationships. She sees that the camp director's sense of his reputation was contingent on "a rule and he couldn't break it"; thus, again, she makes a psychologically astute comment about the internalization of rules and standards. She also alludes to her faith in the protective power of a system of justice, when she says that the camp director could intimidate her and hurt her feelings but he "can't beat me up or anything." And we hear Tanya's resistance to oppressive authority in the form of the "callous" camp director who plays by the rules without exception: "People," Tanya says firmly, "are more important than rules."

As listeners, we are struck not only by Tanya's courage and ability to stay with what she knows about relationships in the face of pressure to not know—to not see and hear—but also by her clarity about her own thoughts and feelings and her sophisticated knowledge of the social world. She says the following of her decision to act on behalf of her cousin: "It wasn't my feeling, my cousin's, but he was, like, really close, but I wasn't feeling what he was feeling, but I did have a little empathy, but not that much. . . . But he was, like, very miserable and I almost felt like he did in a way, so I did, I did go up because I felt miserable having him feel miserable." Here, Tanya makes what would seem, given most descriptions of child development, an astonishing distinction for a twelve-year-old: between experiencing empathy—that is, feeling another's feelings—and responding to another person's feelings with feelings of her own.

Using this method to listen to Tanya's interview narrative at age thirteen (a process that we have abbreviated here because of space limitations), we hear her tell a very different story of relational conflict. Tanya tells a story about feeling trapped in a scene that is not of her own making, which is not what she wants. She describes the conflict in her own terms: "One friend I have and she is supposedly my best friend, you know, and I don't talk to her, because like everybody hates her in class. . . . I mean I don't even like her." The dilemma, Tanya says, is "that I don't like this girl at all, that I absolutely hate her, but I don't know how to act because I have to be nice."

Surprised already by what appears to be a change in Tanya's voice, we listen a second time to her story, attending to the way she speaks about herself in this relational drama. We now hear Tanya's ambivalence ("and I can't say anything to her, because she'll be hurt, so I have no idea what to do"); we hear her speak and then retract what she has said ("this is me, not really"); we witness a sharp increase in her use of the phrase "I don't know" as she wonders what she feels and thinks, what she can know and speak about.

Listening for the relational voices of love and justice, we now hear what sounds like a series of fraudulent relationships based on Tanya's desire not to hurt or upset anyone—her "friend," her friend's mother and sister, and Tanya's mother and sister, who are all friends. Unable to speak about what she feels, Tanya describes a false and "suffocating" closeness that feels like "being married" to someone she does not love. Unspoken, unvoiced, and thus taken out of relationship, her thoughts and feelings have come to seem out of proportion and out of perspective and thus impossible to bring into relationship with others. What she wants to say now is to her unspeakable: "I hate you. Please leave me alone." What she wishes for openly is an end to conflict. Unlike at age twelve when she spoke clearly about herself and her knowledge, and distinguished between what she knows from experience and what authorities say is the case, now Tanya seems to have taken in the conventional, authoritative voice of the culture and is modeling herself on the image of the perfectly caring girl. Giving over the evidence of her own experience—that she and her "friend" are both suffering in this idealized form of relationship—Tanya struggles to authorize, to even identify, her thoughts and feelings. This shift in Tanya's voice over time is, in fact, exemplary of a loss of voice, a struggle for self-authorization, and a move from real to idealized relationships characteristic of the girls to whom we have listened in childhood and adolescence (see Brown, 1989, in press a, in press b; Brown and Gilligan, 1990; Gilligan, 1990).

With our Guide to Listening we draw attention not only to the powerful act of one person interpreting—"naming"—the experience of another but also to the implications of such an act for those who tell psychologists stories about their lives. A relational practice of psychology moves beyond a revisionary interpretation of voices or texts. Such interpretation, in fact, ought to mark only the beginning of a dialogue, the initial move by the listener toward the forming of questions, and ultimately toward a relationship in which both people speak and listen to one another. Rather than focusing on objects to be studied or people to be treated, judged, tested, or assessed, we speak about authentic relationships (that is, relationships in which both people have the opportunity to authorize their thoughts and feelings)—relationships that are as open and mutual as possible, in which partially formed thoughts and strong feelings can be expressed and heard. In creating a method that allows for (and encourages) a polyphony of voices, we cannot, in a relational practice of psychology, cut off or appropriate the voice of the person speaking, especially if her voice is discordant with our own. A shift from encouraging (enforcing) consensus or agreement to engaging diversity creates the possibility for real rather than fraudulent relationships with those whom we engage in our work.

We spoke with Tanya over the course of five years in formal interview settings. And during that time we listened and interpreted and wrote about the changes that we heard in the way she spoke about herself and her relationships. Since then we have been in dialogue with Tanya. Our relationship with her has moved forward and changed; we have learned from her and she has learned from us. In the course of a day-long retreat in which we met with her eleventh-grade class to discuss this research, and after talking with us about her response to a paper (Brown and Gilligan, 1990) in which we wrote in detail about her interviews, Tanya wrote us a letter: "At first I was overcome with a helpless feeling of self-exposure," she said. "I was struck, for it never occurred to me that what I had been saying for the past five years of interviews was of any importance. . . . It was an odd feeling to see my voice in quotes."

Tanya then conversed with us about our interpretation of the changes in her life. She told us of her dismay when at fifteen she was asked to write an essay called "Who Am I?" and she realized that she did not know. Unhappy with her "fascination with the perfect girl" and her "fraudulent view" of herself (phrases from our paper that she felt resonated with her feelings about herself), Tanya spoke of a "voice inside" her that "has been muffled": "The voice that stands up for what I believe in has been buried deep inside of me."

Tanya, whose relational world seemed to us to have darkened over time, continues to surprise us with her resilience, her determination to be heard clearly, her perceptiveness, and her ongoing struggle with conventional feminine ideals. "I do not want the image of a 'perfect girl' to hinder myself from being a truly effective human being," she writes, "yet, I still want to be nice, and I never want to cause any problems."

Conclusion

We began this chapter with four questions about voice that we believe are key to a practice of psychology that is a practice of relationship and a practice of resistance: Whose voice? In what body? Telling what story about relationships? In what societal and cultural framework? We introduced, as central to such a practice of psychology, a relational method—a way of listening that is responsive to these questions, that is attentive to the particular voice of a person speaking, that asks how does that person speak about herself, and that distinguishes the voices of convention that carry gender stereotypes, as well as other norms and values, from relational voices that carry people's desire for closeness or connection and their strong wish to be treated with fairness and respect. We used this method to listen to Tanya, at ages twelve and thirteen, talk about herself and her relationships. We ended with Tanya's wish not to muffle her voice or bury her thoughts and feelings, and thus to be in honest or authentic rather than false relationships with others.

A relational psychology informed by literary theory, by the insights of feminist literary critics, and by clinical insights about psychodynamic processes—that is, a voiced, resonant, resistant psychology—offers an opening, a way of rendering the relational nature of human life. But as psychologists working with people rather than, say, as literary critics interpreting texts, we have to ask why, as Tanya moves from age twelve to age thirteen, does speaking about what she feels and thinks in her relationships, once so simple and genuine for her, become so fraught with difficulty and danger? As we saw, Tanya struggles to hold on to her experience—to know what she knows and to speak in her own voice, to bring her knowledge into the world in which she lives—in the face of authorities and conventions that would otherwise muffle her voice or bury her knowledge. As psychologists who are women, who were once girls, we struggle to hold on to what we know about relationships and feelings, about psyches and bodies, about political and social realities, in a culture where these (our) voices have been trivialized, dismissed, or devalued. By so doing we hope to use our authority and power to enable girls' and women's voices to be heard and engaged openly in relationship—to encourage the open trouble of political resistance, an insistence on knowing what one knows and a willingness to be outspoken, rather than to collude in a silence that fosters the corrosive suffering of psychological resistance, a reluctance to know, and a fear that such knowledge, if spoken, will endanger relationships and threaten survival.

Appendix: Tanya's (Age Twelve) Interview Narrative

INTERVIEWER: Can you tell me a situation where you faced a moral conflict, you had to make a decision, but you weren't sure what you should do?

TANYA: When we were at camp, I went to camp with my sister and my cousin, and he was really young. He was like maybe seven, and he got really, really homesick. It was overnight. And he was like, always crying at night and stuff. And we had this camp guide who was really tough and I was kind of afraid of him, it was like two years ago and I was really afraid of him. And he said, "Nobody's allowed to use the phone." And so my cousin really wanted to call his parents.

INTERVIEWER: Yeah.

TANYA: And it was kind of up to me to go ask the guy if he could. So, either, like, I got bawled out by this guy and asked, or I didn't do anything about it. And he was my cousin, so I had to help him. So I went, so I asked the guy if he could use the phone, and he started giving me this lecture about how there shouldn't be homesickness in this camp. And I said, "Sorry, but he's only seven."

INTERVIEWER: Yeah!

TANYA: And he was really young, and so he finally got to use the phone. So he used the phone, and then we had a camp meeting, and, um, the guy started saying, "Any kid here who gets homesick shouldn't be here." And he didn't say my cousin's name, but he was, like, almost in tears.

INTERVIEWER: Oh, and your cousin was there when he said that? Oh, that wasn't very nice.

TANYA: Yeah. It was really mean.

INTERVIEWER: When you were in this situation, you knew the camp counselor had this policy that you couldn't call, but you also knew that you wanted to help your cousin out. What kinds of things did you consider in thinking about what to do?

TANYA: Well, mostly that, first of all, what was right and wrong.

INTERVIEWER: Um hum.

TANYA: And the right thing was to go because it was for my cousin's good, you know.

INTERVIEWER: Um hum.

TANYA: And he wasn't going to die or anything, but, you know, he's like afraid to go to camp now, because he's like nine now.

INTERVIEWER: Yeah.

TANYA: And he's like, he doesn't want to go back.

INTERVIEWER: Hmm.

TANYA: And so I, like I said, "This guy can, he can intimidate me, but he can't beat me up or anything."

INTERVIEWER: Yeah.

TANYA: And I, I'll realize that that's just the way he is, but I have to do this, so. I mean, it might be wro- . . . he might say no, but it can't hurt asking.

INTERVIEWER: Uh huh. So, can you think of what was the conflict for you when you were trying to decide between, um, between the two options?

TANYA: Just to either keep on my cousin for the week, you know, just help him out.

INTERVIEWER: Um hum.

TANYA: Or have him, like the thing he wanted to do was go home.

INTERVIEWER: Yeah.

TANYA: But, I'm sure, I was sure he wouldn't be able to do that, so if he just talked to his mom, he did feel better.

INTERVIEWER: Okay.

TANYA: But the conflict was that like, it was like he was my cousin you know and we've always been kind of close, and either I help, helped him out or I helped my, or I didn't, like that was for him, or I couldn't go for myself because I didn't want to be like, I was really afraid of that guy, and it was me saving myself or saving him.

INTERVIEWER: Right.

TANYA: So I mean, nothing bad was going to happen to me.

INTERVIEWER: Okay.

TANYA: So I realized that it was worth, like, letting him talk to his parents.

INTERVIEWER: Do you think it was the right thing to do?

TANYA: Yeah.

INTERVIEWER: Why?

TANYA: Why? Because he felt a lot better and even though the guy was, was like giving us a lecture and getting really mean, he was, he was like, he let us use the phone, so I guess he did kind of realize you know cause, my cousin was screaming, has nightmares, and it was really bad, he was with all his friends, so he let him use the phone, but still, I mean I would never see that guy again, you know, if I didn't go back to that camp, but I lived, like my cousin lives seven minutes away from us, so I lived with my cousin, but I would never see that guy again.

INTERVIEWER: I see, okay. So that factored into it, that you were going to see your cousin over and over and over.

TANYA: Yeah, so . . .

INTERVIEWER: Okay. What was at stake for you in the dilemma?

TANYA: Mostly just like kind of like the ego, you know, it's like nothing physically and nothing that anybody else would see. It's just like my feelings being hurt and I hate being yelled at, so . . .

INTERVIEWER: Ah, okay. All right, um, and then what was at stake for the other people involved?

TANYA: The camp director, nothing, but my cousin, just kind a like, to be able to feel better, you know.

INTERVIEWER: Um hum.

TANYA: He was like feeling really, really low. He wasn't being able to have any fun and he paid for it, so he had to do something and he was just like really bad. He was like almost sick, you know. That's why I guess they call it homesick, but.

INTERVIEWER: Right. Well now, why do you think there was nothing at stake for the camp director?

TANYA: Because, well I'm sure there was, but you know the way I saw it at that time was this guy is like a big bully and he can have anything the way he wants it. So you know I don't, I guess it was kind of big letting, giving in for him, you know.

INTERVIEWER: Ah huh.

TANYA: And I guess that kind of showed that he did, he was thinking, I know he was now, but before I didn't. But I was really surprised at him letting him use the phone, but he goes on, see his, like, his reputation, you know, see that was a rule and he couldn't break it, but he said, "Yes, but" and then he started giving us the lecture.

INTERVIEWER: All right, okay. So how did you feel about it?

TANYA: How did I feel?

INTERVIEWER: Um hum.

TANYA: I felt good, but I felt really bad when the camp director went out and said that in the meeting.

INTERVIEWER: Yeah.

TANYA: I was just like, but I did something for him, my cousin, and it's kind of like a victory, you know, it's like you won over this guy, so be happy.

INTERVIEWER: Oh, okay. Even if he did act like a creep the next day or whatever?

TANYA: Yeah.

INTERVIEWER: Do you think there is another way to see the problem, from anybody else's perspective?

TANYA: Yeah, I'm sure, I don't know what it was, but the camp director had another point of view. He was probably, like, "kids always get homesick and what difference does it make, he's not going to die," you know, but he wasn't that kid.

INTERVIEWER: Yeah.

TANYA: And so he, he had a totally different point of view from my cousin and I.

INTERVIEWER: Um hum.

TANYA: And then like my friends probably, you know, they knew about it, and they were like, "I understand but it's not, why does he cry all the time," you know.

INTERVIEWER: Yeah.

TANYA: It's like, either you feel it, like all the way, or you just, like, recognize it, you know?

INTERVIEWER: Sure, sure. It sounds like the camp director wasn't even doing either of those two.

TANYA: I know, he was really callous.

INTERVIEWER: Yeah. Okay, so when you think back over the conflict that you just described, do you think you learned anything from it?

TANYA: Well, you know, it's obvious that was right.

INTERVIEWER: It's obvious that you were right?

TANYA: No, yeah, the decision was right, you know.

INTERVIEWER: Now, why is it obvious?

TANYA: It's obvious because it's, no it isn't, but it is for me. It might not be for you or somebody else, but it's helping out my cousin and that camp director, you know, it's a rule, but people are more important than rules, you know. So he was just a little kid, you know, and they were trying out things, and the camp director, they were saying, "Well, we're here to help our kids, to make them have fun," but my cousin wasn't having fun, he was just contradicting the whole slogan.

INTERVIEWER: Yeah.

TANYA: You know.

INTERVIEWER: Right . . .

TANYA: So it wasn't for that, and it was just like, I guess if you did ask somebody they would say, "Oh that is right," but then you say well the answer, and "I don't know . . . the reason, you know."

INTERVIEWER: But you felt it was right?

TANYA: Yeah, I felt it was right.

INTERVIEWER: Do you consider this situation you described a moral problem?

TANYA: What's that?

INTERVIEWER: Well, I don't want to define it, because then you have my definition. But, um, oh, okay, let me try this one. What does morality mean to you? When you hear that word, what does that mean?

TANYA: Morality? Um, probably like, it has to do with the person . . . Oh! We did this in English the other day.

INTERVIEWER: [Laughs] So I hear.

TANYA: Um morality was, it's like the difference between right and wrong, you know, and it's when the person like chooses the right thing, it's like, in the long run, or, um, like even in that little experience or that little incident, but, um, it's just like what's deep down when you think about it is going to be right, and what's going to help you out or help the other person out, and then the conflict is what is a decision, but it's like not going to do anything, it's just gonna maybe make things, life, easier.

INTERVIEWER: Okay, well, then I could ask you then what is a moral problem for you? What do you think makes a moral problem?

TANYA: Maybe when, you know, it has something to do with people or your friends, or just like even a dog or something, and it's when you know the difference between right and wrong but it's going to be easier, I mean, it's like if you're lazy, you know it's easier to take the wrong one, so it's like a decision.

INTERVIEWER: Okay. Do you think the situation, the story with your cousin and the camp director, would that be considered a moral problem for you?

TANYA: Yeah, because I could have gotten out of it easily, you know, and it wasn't my feeling, my cousin's, but he was, like, really close, but I wasn't feeling what he was feeling, so like I did have a little empathy, but you know not that much. So, either like I could have gotten out of it and said, "I'm not going up to that camp director, you go up yourself," to my cousin, but you know he was, like, very miserable and I almost felt like he did in a way, so I did, I did go up you know because I felt miserable having him feel miserable.

INTERVIEWER: Right. I bet.

References

Bakhtin, M. M. *The Dialogic Imagination.* (C. Emerson and M. Holquist, trans.) Austin: University of Texas Press, 1981.

Brown, L. M. "Narratives of Relationship: The Development of a Care Voice in Girls Ages 7 to 16." Unpublished doctoral dissertation, Graduate School of Education, Harvard University, 1989.

Brown, L. M. "A Problem of Vision: The Development of Voice and Relational Knowledge in Girls Ages 7 to 16." *Women's Studies Quarterly,* in press a.

Brown, L. M. "Telling a Girl's Life: Self-Authorization as a Form of Resistance." *Women and Therapy,* in press b.

Brown, L. M., Argyris, D., Attanucci, J., Bardige, B., Gilligan, C., Johnston, K., Miller,

B., Osborne, R., Tappan, M. B., Ward, J., Wiggins, G., and Wilcox, D. *A Guide to Reading Narratives of Conflict and Choice for Self and Relational Voice*. Monograph No. 1. Cambridge, Mass.: Project on Women's Psychology and Girls' Development, Harvard Graduate School of Education, 1988.

Brown, L. M., Debold, E., Tappan, M. B., and Gilligan, C. "Reading Narratives of Conflict and Choice for Self and Moral Voice: A Relational Method." In W. Kurtines and J. Gewirtz (eds.), *Handbook of Moral Behavior and Development: Theory, Research, and Application*. Hillsdale, N.J.: Erlbaum, 1991.

Brown, L. M., and Gilligan, C. "The Psychology of Women and the Development of Girls." Paper presented at the biennial meetings of the Society for Research on Adolescence, Atlanta, Georgia, March 1990.

Brown, L. M., Tappan, M. B., Gilligan, C., Miller, B., and Argyris, D. "Reading for Self and Moral Voice: A Method for Interpreting Narratives of Real-Life Moral Conflict and Choice." In M. J. Packer and R. Addison (eds.), *Entering the Circle: Hermeneutic Investigation in Psychology*. Albany: State University of New York Press, 1989.

Burke, K. *A Grammar of Motives*. Berkeley and Los Angeles: University of California Press, 1969.

Fetterley, J. *The Resisting Reader: A Feminist Approach to American Fiction*. Bloomington: Indiana University Press, 1978.

Gilligan, C. *In a Different Voice: Psychological Theory and Women's Development*. Cambridge, Mass.: Harvard University Press, 1982.

Gilligan, C. "Joining the Resistance: Psychology, Politics, Girls, and Women." *Michigan Quarterly Review*, 1990, *29*, 501–536.

Gilligan, C., and Attanucci, J. "Two Moral Orientations: Gender Differences and Similarities." *Merrill-Palmer Quarterly*, 1988, *34*, 223–237.

Gilligan, C., Brown, L. M., and Rogers, A. "Psyche Embedded: A Place for Body, Relationships, and Culture in Personality Theory." In A. Rabin, R. Zucker, R. Emmons, and S. Frank (eds.), *Studying Persons and Lives*. New York: Springer, 1990.

Gilligan, C., Ward, J., and Taylor, J. (eds.). *Mapping the Moral Domain*. Cambridge, Mass.: Harvard University Press, 1988.

Gilligan, C., and Wiggins, G. "The Origins of Morality in Early Childhood Relationships." In J. Kagan and S. Lamb (eds.), *The Emergence of Morality in Young Children*. Chicago: University of Chicago Press, 1987.

Millett, K. *Sexual Politics*. Garden City, N.J.: Doubleday, 1970.

Rich, A. "Vesuvius at Home: The Power of Emily Dickinson." In A. Rich, *On Lies, Secrets, and Silence*. New York: Norton, 1979a.

Rich, A. "When We Dead Awaken: Writing as Re-Vision." In A. Rich, *On Lies, Secrets, and Silence*. New York: Norton, 1979b.

Rogers, A., and Gilligan, C. *Translating the Language of Adolescent Girls: Themes of Moral Voice and Stages of Ego Development*. Monograph No. 6. Cambridge, Mass.: Project on Women's Psychology and Girls' Development, Harvard Graduate School of Education, 1988.

Schweickart, P. "Reading Ourselves: Toward a Feminist Theory of Reading." In E. Flynn and P. Schweickart (eds.), *Gender and Reading: Essays on Readers, Texts, and Contexts*. Baltimore, Md.: Johns Hopkins University Press, 1986.

Lyn Mikel Brown is assistant professor of education and co-chair of the education department at Colby College, Waterville, Maine. She is also research associate with the Project on Women's Psychology and Girls' Development at the Harvard Graduate School of Education. Her research interests focus on girls' psychological development, girls' education, and feminist methods.

Carol Gilligan is professor of education at the Harvard Graduate School of Education and director of the Project on Women's Psychology and Girls' Development.

While a "hermeneutics of narrative" can show us how people
understand their world in complex, socially available, organized
ways, and how as researchers we, too, actively construe as we try
to understand other people, a "hermeneutics of action" is needed
to overcome our addiction to the belief that knowing *the world*
is our primary kind of engagement with it.

Interpreting Stories, Interpreting Lives: Narrative and Action in Moral Development Research

Martin J. Packer

Consider the following brief improvisatory narrative, told to a kindergarten teacher by a five-year-old named Ann, who is outraged that her peers are not granting her the turn she has requested in their play at jumping through a hoop: "You know what? I already asked first, um, and Laurie just came along and asked and then Kathryn said that Laurie's after her because I asked first."

Here is a recounting of one or more real events that do not logically presuppose or entail one another, with a continuant subject, constituting a whole, communicated by a narrator to a narratee (Prince, 1987, p. 58). But the sequencing of events is only one aspect of this narrative. The narrative points to a wrong-doing and grows out of a breakdown in practice that this wrong-doing constitutes. It is directed to a specific other in order to appeal for an intervention, the character of which is clear, though implicit. Furthermore, just prior to going over to the teacher with her narrative, Ann stomps her foot and announces to her peers, "Well I ASKED FIRST! I'm telling!"; it is evident that she knows that in "telling" her story she is adopting a confrontational moral stance. A reading of even this short a narrative gives us a sense of the moral terms in which she grasps events; but, in addition, when we place this episode within the larger whole from which it is drawn, we can articulate details of the practical project in which Ann is engaged, and the social order of which she partakes.

It is usually evident when speech (like Ann's account) and writing have a narrative organization and so need to be interpreted in a way that is sensitive to the special characteristics of narrative. Human activity is less obviously in need of such treatment, but several lines of thought lead us to see that the activity also requires interpretation of a similar kind. In part this is because the narrative mode of explanation is an alternative to logical and causal explanations of action (what Bruner [1986, 1987] calls the paradigmatic mode). But while human activity is certainly an endless topic of narrative explication, this feature speaks only to the *possibility* of an interpretive approach to action.

This chapter explores reasons for thinking that the interpretation of action has a *necessary* part in our research, albeit one that is generally covered over. Narrative texts can be considered in terms of the characters and plot they portray, as schematic organizations providing cues to an actively engaged reader, or as situated discourse that has become enduring by virtue of being fixed in written form. Each of these facets provides fruit to a narrative approach to moral development research. Narratology and reader response theory are discussed first, and then the implications of viewing narrative as, first of all, a mode of action are considered. The argument is that the interpretation of narrative texts can show us how people understand their world in complex, socially available, organized ways, and how as researchers we, too, actively construe as we try to understand people's stories. But only by interpreting the role of narratives in ongoing everyday action can we overcome our virtual addiction to the belief that our primary kind of engagement with the world is *knowing* it. This leads to a discussion of Heidegger's hermeneutic ontology as an account of the way that interpretation and narrative have their roots in practical breakdowns and contradictions. Finally, in shifting the emphasis of our research toward the way narratives are situated in practice, we are led to a rethinking of moral development, particularly the end point of that development.

Narratives and Narratology

Narrative is the recounting of events; a narrative provides a way of coherently linking these events in time. The power of narrative to organize and explain has recently been praised by historians (for example, White, 1981), psychiatrists (for example, Spence, 1982), and moral philosophers (for example, Jonsen and Toulmin, 1988), while new species of narrative analysis in literary studies enjoy vogue status throughout the humanities. Philosophical analyses of narrative (for example, Ricoeur, 1984, 1985, 1988) grant it, if possible, even greater power, as the unique place of a mimesis of life that is a necessary part of any attempt to understand ourselves and the world in which we live. Given this widespread surge of interest in narrative, it is no surprise that psychology, too, is witnessing an increasing appreciation of the role of narratives in human affairs, and the use of narrative methods for analysis of interviews and other textual materials (see Sarbin, 1986). For instance, Mishler (1986) has drawn our attention to the implications of the fact that interviews are not simple question-and-answer sequences whereby factual information is obtained from a research "subject" but instead are human interactions in social settings. As such, they produce discourse with narrative organization, structured to achieve particular concrete social ends (see Suchman and Jordan, 1990). Yet, these narratives have typically been edited out as irrelevant.

The most straightforward approach to the analysis of a narrative attends to its organization on the level of character and plot. Classical structuralist literary theory is of this type. Structuralist analyses distinguish between the two planes of *story* (content, or what is narrated) and *discourse* (expression, or the narrating). Story is typically analyzed in terms of elements such as *actants* and *events* (Greimas and Courtes, 1976), or *roles* and *moves* (Propp, 1968). Discourse, in turn, can be further differentiated into *substance* (medium) and *form* (the connected set of narrative statements). Discursive form is then considered in terms of such features as the chronological order of presentation of events, point of view, pacing of action, and nature of any commentary by the narrator.

At this level of analysis, narrative is a distinctive mode of reporting one's experience of the world. Much can be learned by attending to the characters and the events of which narratives speak. Day's (this volume) description of the characters that inhabit the dramatic stage on which moral decisions are made demonstrates the value of such an analysis. Day takes his informants' reports on members of internal audiences such as the Incredible Hulk, a grandfather, and a close friend at face value, as veridical accounts of inner experience.

Such an analysis is often a useful exercise for sharpening one's understanding of what is going on in a narrative (which is why it forms the basis for the first of the four "listenings" or readings in Brown and Gilligan, this volume). What is missing from narratology, however, is any sense of the *work of reading* that every text requires. Narratology treats the elements of character and plot as though they have an autonomous existence. But these figures and events do not spring fully formed from the page; a little reflection shows that the reading of any text must, for instance, draw on what is *not* said as well as what is and so points up the importance of the text's appeal to the reader's expectations, to stylistic conventions, and to a tacit understanding of society and culture. This appeal is most evident when the text is a work of fiction, but it is equally true when we consider such texts as interview transcripts or transcripts of everyday conversation. The researcher plays an active role in interpreting this kind of material, too. How best can we identify and understand that activity, and its inevitable part in the research enterprise?

The school of literary theory in which the active role of the reader has been most elucidated is reader response theory, also known as reception theory and reception aesthetics. This approach to the analysis of literary texts (and, by extension, to other material with a textual character) is a French and German development of Gadamer's (1985) hermeneutics. The chief figures here are Wolfgang Iser (1978), Roman Ingarden (1973), Hans Jauss (1977, 1982), and Stanley Fish (1989). Unlike approaches built on the belief that a text can be studied in isolation, as an independent entity in its own right, reader response theorists maintain that it is essential to analyze as well the active role played by the reader, who is considered to be in a constructive engagement with the text: making assumptions, drawing inferences, and constructing interpretations. The text is seen as providing a reader with a series of cues or instructions; it is made up of a sequence of *schemata* that provide general directions to a reader. Furthermore, any text provides only incomplete information; it is full of gaps that the reader must fill or bridge by drawing on knowledge of the world, and of literary conventions, that is not present in the text itself. This is one reason for the phenomenon of textual ambiguity; most texts can support alternative interpretations, and the reader must shift from one perspective to another, selecting and organizing, excluding some elements and foregrounding others, in order to build up the integrated interpretation that constitutes a "reading" of the text. This plurivocality also becomes apparent when texts are read in cultures and times different from those of their production. Jauss (1977, 1982), in particular, has emphasized the need to consider the *horizon* of both text and reader. Every text becomes newly situated in the cultural context that its reader occupies, a context determined by factors such as the reader's gender, ethnicity, class, and age. At the same time, every text has an *implied reader*: Its cues and codes reflect a sense of its likely audience.

An example of an approach to the study of moral development that is in consort with reader response theory is provided by the work of Lyn Mikel Brown, Carol Gilligan, and their colleagues (see Brown and Gilligan, this volume; also Brown, Tappan, Gilligan, Miller, and Argyris, 1989). These researchers emphasize the active character of reading in their analyses of interview narratives of real-life moral conflicts. Brown, Debold, Tappan, and Gilligan (1991, p. 27) describe their approach as both a reader response method and a feminist method: "Such a focus on the relationship between the reader's and the narrator's perspective directly challenges the strive toward 'objectivity'—a disembodied voice and a detached point of view that characterizes traditional empiricist and rationalist approaches to psychological inquiry."

Reader response theory, then, draws our attention, as researchers, to the active role we play in making sense of interview material. Reader and narrative are in a dynamic interplay that cannot be grasped by traditional views of the researcher as ideally detached and neutral, free from preconceptions and prejudgments. On the contrary, preconceptions of a variety of kinds play an essential role in the comprehension of textual narratives. (Typically, in reader response theory, what the reader brings to the text is described as a matter of assumptions, expectations, and so on. But to describe the text in such cognitive terms is to neglect the ontological level of a reader's involvement with the text, as discussed here shortly.) In research on moral development these preconceptions include assumptions about the distinguishing characteristics of "the moral," its relationship to putatively nonmoral domains, the relations among cognitive, affective, and conative aspects of morality, and so forth (see Tappan, 1990). The extent to which such preconceptions can be explicitly chosen, and the degree to which they can be corrected in the course of research, are, needless to say, very complex questions (see Packer, 1989).

Narrative as Representation, Narrative as Action

The dynamic relationship between reader and text is only one of several relationships that the narrative text has with the circumstances of its production and of its consumption. These relationships, analyzed in detail by Ricoeur (1979), have their roots in the origins of written text in spoken discourse, which designates its speaker and hearer and makes reference to its location in space and time. Discourse designates its speaker by devices such as personal pronouns, and the meaning of its words expresses the speaker's intention; it addresses a specific audience; it is located in time as a fleeting material event; and it refers ostensively to an actual situation common to the interlocutors. Thus, a written text is discourse that has been "fixed." ("All writing is . . . a kind of alienated speech, and its signs need to be transformed back into speech and meaning"; Gadamer, 1985, p. 354.) When discourse is fixed, as writing, its relations to speaker, audience, place, and time are not eliminated but modified. First, the text is no longer fleeting; this permanence is, after all, a primary purpose of writing. Second, the text's tie to the author is distended and complicated: "The text's career escapes the finite horizon lived by its author" (Ricoeur, 1979, p. 78). Third, the text refers now to a world of nonsituational references; it opens up a new way of seeing the world. And, finally, the text explodes the narrowness of the dialogical relation; it is now addressed to an audience that it creates.

What is the significance of Ricoeur's (1979) analysis for the study of moral development? First, it highlights characteristics of the material we study that are largely taken for granted. When we interview our research participants, we unthinkingly capitalize on the traits of narrative text. When we include such transcripts in our published reports, we rely on the fact that these texts can be read by people who have known neither the events narrated nor the persons narrating them. Honey (1987, p. 80) argues that the interview itself involves forms of fixing and distancing, such that it "is not a conversation in the usual sense of the word; rather, the interview is a spoken text." Whether or not one agrees with this contention, most interviews go through the additional step of being tape-recorded and transcribed and are certainly fixed by this process.

Second, consideration of what happens when speech is fixed as a text raises the question of the aim of a textual interpretation. When we interpret a narrative text about an everyday moral conflict, what are we trying to do? Ricoeur argues convincingly that textual interpretation can never be a return to the author's intention. The "problem of interpretation"—that is to say, the need for clarification that motivates interpretation in the first place—is not due to the impenetrability of the mental experience of the author, though that is indeed impenetrable. Rather, it is due to the "specific plurivocity" of all texts: the way they are open to several readings, each from a different perspective, because of the holistic construal that the reading involves, as parts are read in the light of a preliminary sense of the whole. When we interpret a narrative about moral conflict, then, we must avoid the psychologistic trap of trying to identify the narrator's subjective experience of events: the equivalent of the author's intention.

The third, and perhaps most important, way in which Ricoeur's analysis of the origins of text in discourse has significance for the study of moral development is that it suggests that we can move from conceiving of narratives solely as a mode of *representation* to considering them as, at the same time, a mode of *action*. Ricoeur's purpose in considering the traits of discourse that has been fixed as text is broader than simply to better understand texts; it is to reconsider questions about the *objects* and *methodology* of the social sciences. *Action* is the proper object, and *interpretation* the proper method, but "meaningful action is an object for science only under the conditions of a kind of objectification which is equivalent to the fixation of a discourse by writing. . . . This objectification is made *possible* by some inner traits of action . . . which make doing a kind of utterance" (Ricoeur, 1979, pp. 80–81). By viewing action in this way, we have a means of overcoming the apparent "methodological paradox" of the human sciences, which, as Dilthey (1976) framed it, is that the explanation (*Erklaren*) of human life seems to require objectifications that make no appeal to understanding (*Verstehen*). Put briefly, a text is a kind of object, but one that still requires exegesis and interpretation. As such, it provides the space for a dialectical interplay of explanation and understanding. The "objectivity" of the text provides us with the basis for a new understanding of the human sciences, because this objectivity makes possible a kind of "explaining" that is not derived from the natural sciences.

So, while a hermeneutics of narrative texts can show us how people represent their world in complex, socially available, organized ways, and how as researchers we, too, actively construe as we try to understand other people, narrative also provides us with a route to the study of action. The study of action has been neglected in moral development research, and I maintain that a hermeneutics of action—undertaken through narratives and other modes of fixing—is needed to overcome our addiction to the belief that *knowing* the world is our primary kind of engagement with it.

Let me elaborate this claim with reference to the reader response method described above. Despite the strengths of their step away from the structuralist approach to moral development, Gilligan, Brown, and their colleagues have been, at least until recently, primarily interested, like Kohlberg, in the *epistemic* subject: They studied an interview transcript not simply as a description of a specific event or experience but also for the *terms* in which a person construes everyday moral conflicts. Specifically, Kohlberg (1981, 1984) aims at the rational reconstruction of a moral competence underlying the subject's reasoning about a moral dilemma; Gilligan (1982) aims to characterize the moral orientation by which a situation is understood, and by which a moral problem is constructed. In both cases what is sought is the *framework* within which events are organized, not a person's intentions and motives. The differences between these two approaches concern the underlying beliefs about the character of the framework: for Kohlberg it is a unitary system of unfolding stages of principles of justice; for Gilligan it is a gendered voice with which the vulnerable self may succeed or fail in aligning. Moreover, the voices of care and justice that Gilligan distinguishes are not subjective in the sense of being idiosyncratic, personal ways of construing the world; they are possible ways of structuring subjectivity that have been made available to all of us by our common culture.

The reader response approach has downplayed both the concrete events of the narrated story and the narrator's conduct in recounting that story, focusing instead on the "way" the story was told. The result has a lingering taste of structuralism: Care and justice were presented as transcendental frameworks within which the world is construed and events made sense of. If there was a danger here, it was that the voices were treated as ahistorical, acultural, natural, and inevitable, just as Kohlberg's stages often have been treated. (For the importance of locating the moral voices of justice and care in their sociocultural and historical context, see Tappan, 1991.) The focus was still epistemological, even though the epistemology was informed by considerations of engagement and by a sociopolitical stance (see Brown, 1986). Our attention, therefore, was still drawn to the narrator as representer *of* the world rather than as agent *in* the world, as primarily active *mentally,* shaping *representations* of the world but not the world itself. What was missing, it seems, was a deeper appreciation of the way that the subject is always practically engaged, and of both the fact and character of this engagement.

The approach that Brown and Gilligan describe in this volume, however, moves much more clearly toward this latter kind of analysis. They write of the political character of their research questions and their research method, of the way that a "resisting listener" raises questions about power and authority in an androcentric society. As a result, Brown and Gilligan now show us that narratives do more than express the perspective of their narrator. First, the story telling itself is a response to being interviewed, which is a social event whose meaning and significance has been negotiated, explicitly or otherwise, by the parties involved. Second, the textual contradictions that Brown and Gilligan draw to our attention, and would have us read for, represent real existential conflicts, unresolved not only in the interview narrative but also, and more significantly, in the world. As Ricoeur (1979) puts it, the interview narrative points to a world by means of nonostensive reference, since the events narrated are of the past, but in so doing it also directs the reader's attention to "boundary situations" that it typifies. Struggles with illegitimate authority, matters of life and death, these human situations are referred to by the text by virtue of its independence, what Ricoeur calls its "transcendence," from the occasions of its production and the setting it purports to describe. For Brown and Gilligan, then, the situations of greatest significance are those of a young woman's entry into our male-centered culture.

The text of an interview narrative can thus provide us with a new way of looking at things, through a movement from what is *said* to what is *talked about.* We can pay attention to the terms in which people frame events, the terms in which they are understood, but we can also consider the species of events talked about. What difference does this shift in attention make to the study of moral development? With interviews it entails paying more attention to how the narrator represents her own agency in the story and the consequences of her action (this is the kind of analysis addressed in Tappan, this volume). Since with interview material there is a problem of the "duality" of action (the "doing" of telling, and the "doing" told about), the shift also entails a move to action fixed not just in retrospective narratives but also in media such as video recordings (see Packer and Richardson, 1991). And it requires an analysis of the social ontology of human practice.

Hermeneutic Ontology

Heidegger (1962), like Ricoeur, was concerned with the kind of objectification that a human science requires. Heidegger's striking move, central to his analysis, is one that changes the way we think about human existence, action, and knowledge. This move is to place understanding (*Verstehen*) on an ontological instead of an epistemological plane. Understanding, Heidegger proposed, is first and foremost an aspect of our being; to exist as human *is* to understand the world in which we are situated. We do not exist in the world as material entities and then, separately and subsequently, acquire knowledge of our surroundings; our existence *is* an understanding of the world. Our first preliminary indication that this is so comes from our recognition that we are the kind of beings whose beingness is an issue for us; human existence involves or entails an understanding of what it is to be human. From this preliminary inkling of the place of understanding in existence, Heidegger moved systematically to articulate the way our existence is always located in circumstances into which each of us finds we have been thrown, is always an active projecting of possibilities that arise from this situation, and is structured by a temporal stance, a way of unfolding and showing past, present, and future.

In this account understanding is, first and foremost, a way of grasping the entities around us in an active and engaged manner. Through this grasping we comprehend ourselves at the same time. Mostly, these entities, and the network of interrelationships among them, are transparent and invisible to us, but when practice breaks down, the entities and their interrelationships stand out as troublesome. At this point, in our practical deliberations on breakdown, we undertake interpretation, articulating aspects of our project, its objects, and its setting, in order to resume smooth practice (Packer, 1985). Interpretation is the articulation—the laying out and explication—of possibilities that have been projected and have become available in practical understanding.

In this account knowledge is always rooted in, and organized by, our practical engagement in the world. What might appear to be objective knowledge of independent objects' properties, or of formal moral principles, is always, if Heidegger is correct, structured by concerned engagement in practical projects—in the most general analysis, by "care." (Kuhn [1970], among others, is anticipated here; scientific knowledge always operates within a taken-for-granted network of practices, a paradigm, whose operation is transparent and so invisible until anomalies force themselves upon the practitioners of science, and so bring the paradigm to light.)

This account thus shows us the hidden kernel of truth, as well as the distortion, in cognitive accounts of the way preconceptions and assumptions (structures, schemes, scripts) organize our perception and understanding of new phenomena. It is true that we understand the new in terms of what we already know, but more broadly and completely we understand the new in terms of *who we already are*. The locus of operation of "pre-understanding" is therefore at the ontological not the epistemological level, at the level of who we are and what we do, not (or not first) what we know. (This is true of the reading of texts, too, hence the objection raised earlier to overly rational and cognitivist accounts of the reading process, even in hermeneutically informed reader response theory.)

This shift in emphasis in the way we construe knowing and acting has genuinely profound implications for the way we conceive of and study development, including its moral aspects. Foremost, it draws attention to the fact that almost every theory of psychological development has assumed that development is the acquisition and reorganization of knowledge. Even theories like Piaget's and Vygotsky's, which acknowledge the centrality of action in early childhood, assume that development entails a movement away from the sensorimotor toward the abstract and intellectual. Moral development research has made similar assumptions. It would be naive to insist that this emphasis on knowledge over action is simply a theoretical mistake. It is better viewed as a cultural and historical blindness, a systematic misunderstanding that we have of the kind of beings that we are. Substantial problems are the result, which I can only list in part here: the problem of arriving at moral conclusions with real substance (such as the choice of a specific course of action) by means of formal reasoning; the problem that even if a decision is made, it is still detached, both analytically and phenomenologically, from purposive action; and the problem of explaining apparent divergences between competence and performance.

A second implication of Heidegger's account of the structure of human existence as being-in-the-world is the suggestion that development is the transformation, at one and the same time, of three aspects of existence: (1) the subject, as a system of powers and inclinations, (2) the social artifacts and institutions reproduced in human activity, and (3) the mode of concerned engagement in the world. Cognitive accounts of moral development consider only the third of these three, although they confuse it with the first and reduce it to a solely epistemic matter. The details of this account are not to be found, of course, in *Being and Time*, but the possibility of such an analysis is apparent. The study of development in these terms is what is alluded to by the phrase "interpreting lives" in the title of this chapter (see also Freeman, this volume).

Let us consider briefly these three aspects of development. First, Heidegger raises what he calls "the question of the 'who'." We have tended (perhaps since Descartes's positing of the ego cogito, perhaps since the Christian doctrine of the soul) to presume that the subject of development, the psychological subject, is straightforward, self-evident, and unchanging in character. Heidegger, instead, helps us recognize the problematic, open-ended character of the subject. He argues that there is no simple, natural, pregiven self that, if it changes at all, simply unfolds in a logical manner. The subject of human activity can adopt a variety of forms: It has a range of modes available to it, possibilities that are given by the culture and tradition it finds itself in. Heidegger talks of the inauthentic "anyone," of the authentic self, and of an undifferentiated "who": One can imagine others, including the modern "individual" subject to whom we appeal so often (see Berger, Berger, and Kellner, 1973; Taylor, 1989), and a variety of collective subjects. We must attend to transformations of the subject in the course of development, as a changing identity that should not be understood simply as a matter of the reflective knowledge a subject has of itself, as the subject considered only as an object of its own knowledge (see Blasi, 1984). The transformation of the subject involves reflective knowledge, but more primordially it involves the development of powers and inclinations that locate the subject in material relationship to other identities. Identity is a matter of finding a "place" for oneself in society.

Second, human development must mean a transformation of the social artifacts and institutions that call for our concern and engagement. Theories of the formation of the subject are generally far too straightforward, for they do not account for the way subjects transform social resources as they appropriate them. Also, the theories are too mysterious, insofar as the mechanisms of social influence—reinforcement, direct instruction, internalization—are appealed to rather than clearly spelled out. Heidegger's account of human being includes, from the outset, reference to that being's specificity and historicity, but also reference to its active character, constantly pressing forward or projecting into the future. Persons (or groups) take up possibilities from those that their culture and circumstances make available to them, but at the same time they transform these possibilities as they take them up. Only an impoverished psychology, surely, considers human development without reference to the products of human activity. Can Picasso's development as an artist, let alone as a human, be considered by reference only to his theories or beliefs about painting, and not to the actual works of art that he created, considered as replies to the constraints and resources of his time and place?

Third, development entails change in the way that the world is grasped, as a reorganization of practice, not (or not first) of knowledge. Different concerns and new projects characterize children of different ages, and these projects and concerns are not the individual construction of an epistemic subject but instead are grounded in the culturally prescribed circumstances that children find themselves entering: family, forms of schooling, workplace, and so on. These constitute a *ground* from which practical possibilities are made available. In its most immediate guise, this ground is the organized local setting, a totality (albeit not without contradictions) of tools, artifacts, and institutions in which our projects take (their) place. In a deeper analysis it is our culture that makes practical possibilities available, appropriate to the subject's place in it; that subject is never natural or universal but always gendered, ethnic, and classed. Genders, ethnic groups, and social classes are themselves social possibilities that we always find we have already taken up; gender, ethnicity, and class are both modes of embodiment and modes of collectivity. It is in this sense that we belong to history rather than it belonging to us, and that tradition is the deepest ground from which our projects spring (see MacIntyre, 1984, 1988).

A third implication of Heidegger's analysis is that it shows that interpretation is not a special type of analysis necessary for, and restricted to, textual exegesis; it is a mode of comprehension, of grasping the world, rooted in our human way of being in the world. Properly understood, interpretation is a tendency inherent to our way of being. The phenomena to which literary interpretation draws our attention—holism between the text grasped in its entirety and its parts, the progressive articulation from a preliminary reading, the way reading is shaped by anticipation and assumption—find their counterparts, indeed their primordial forms, in our everyday existence as cultural beings.

In the most general terms, then, interpretation illuminates the different aspects of a phenomenon, along with the ground upon which that phenomenon stands out and from which it draws its possibilities. In terms more specific to humans, it describes the possible ways we have of comporting ourselves, and the cultural and historical grounds from which these ways are taken up and transformed. Translated into the terminology of a study of moral development, interpretation entails studying children's ways of acting in, and understanding, their relations with others; the sources of these ways in our culture, viewed as a tradition extended in time; how these ways are transformed as they are taken up; and how they transform the children who appropriate them in action.

Children in a kindergarten playground (see Packer and Richardson, 1991) are situated in a world of artifacts, equipment, and arenas of activity, the organization of which embodies a manifold of cultural possibilities. These possibilities can be recognized in the modes of activity that are sanctioned and those that are not (what counts as hurting others, breaching rights of possession and occupation), the provision of artifacts that are at one and the same time expressively designed for children (as "toys" and "playthings") and miniature copies of implements of the home and the workplace, and the very fact that the playground is a place of play as distinct from study. The playground is the material ground for children's activity, posing preconditions that both constrain that activity and provide powerful resources for it. Children's active "projection" of these possibilities can be seen when they take them up in ways that test and often breach adult expectations, so that the adults must be forever vigilant for these breaches. Girls "marry" girls; "swords" are forged from "shovels"; a "safe" climbing structure becomes a place for daring leaps. Teachers constantly work to correct these misinterpretations of the playground's possibilities.

Seen in these terms, moral development is not a matter of adopting social norms, or constructing rationally compelling ethical principles, or establishing an unproblematic consensus among equals. It is rather a matter of resolving, as best one can, moral obligations that have a history, obligations that reflect and shape a response to the demands—the call—of existence in a world that is fundamentally not of our own making. (This position can be contrasted with most social constructivist positions. Talk of the "social construction of reality" does seem to involve a view of the subject as somehow having taken over the transcendent power of a deity. To say that humans "construct" the world would be the height of hubris except, of course, that all the statement actually means is that our knowledge of the world is socially constructed. Once more, epistemology has been given unquestioned priority.) In other words, Heidegger's analysis draws our attention to the ways in which we unwittingly both hand down and reconfigure cultural tradition in our actions:

> None of us finds himself placed in the radical position of creating the ethical world *ex nihilo*. It is an inescapable aspect of our finite condition that we are born into a world already qualified in an ethical manner. . . . We can perhaps "transvaluate" values, but we can never create them beginning from zero. The passage through tradition has no other justification than this antecedence of the ethical world with regard to every ethical subject. But, on the other hand, we never receive values as we find things. . . . Our interest in emancipation introduces . . . "ethical distance" into our relation to any heritage [Ricoeur, 1973, p. 164].

The radical interpretation that articulates this grounding of morality in tradition takes a narrative form. And simpler, more everyday interpretations can also appear as narratives. To see how narrative grows from action is to see that the relationship between action and narrative is neither a simple one of parallelism, where fixed action has an objectlike structure similar to fixed narrative, nor one of part to whole, where speech is one species of action. In interpretation it first becomes evident that human activity involves a complex system of part-whole relations, is plurivocal, has a complex temporality, makes indexical reference to the circumstances of its production, yet at the same time escapes these circumstances—in short, that its characteristics are those we more readily attribute to narrative texts. But action and narrative are linked dialectically, as two aspects of a whole. When our practice breaks down, narrative enables us to make sense of the difficulty and uncover new courses of action. Narratives can grow from action in this way because human activity always operates within a world that is already interpreted, not explicitly but grasped in a particular manner. (Again, the way a mature science always operates within a taken-for-granted paradigm is a good, and familiar, example.) An effective narrative has the power to bring some aspect of this way that the world is grasped to light, and to show fresh possibilities for action. A persuasive narrative does not aim to make statements about the world that are merely descriptive; it aims to *move* the hearer to action. (Narrative and emotion are closely linked here, hence the emphasis in classical rhetoric on the "pathetic" argument, the component of discourse that moves the audience to action by rousing emotions; Aristotle, 1954. Emotions can be considered a form of interpersonal movement whose power comes from transforming the way the world is grasped; see De Rivera, 1977; Hall and Cobey, 1976.) Only when breakdown proves intransigent do we "step back" and resort to more general and abstract tools such as logical analysis and calculation (Packer, 1985, p. 1084), showing that the narrative mode of explanation undergirds and provides the possibility for the logical explanatory mode.

Finding a Place for Critique

We have considered how narrative can be appreciated and analyzed from several different aspects. Narrative is an organization of events and persons; it is open to different readings, and those readings are active construals; it refers to a world and opens up new ways of looking at that world; hence it opens up new possibilities for action, reflecting the fact that it typically grows out of a breakdown or conflict in practice. We have considered how human existence itself is a way of understanding the world and, as such, contains the origins of a narrative mode of interpretation and explication. Finally, we can consider how narrative, viewed now as enactive as well as representational, points toward a new moral order, and the implications of this view of narrative for the study of moral development.

Attention to narrative promises to resolve a dilemma that presently confronts developmental psychology. To talk of development requires reference to criteria of some kind, yet in the moral realm the choice of criteria seems quite problematic. Appeal to universal, logically compelling ethical principles has been convincingly called into question, as has the notion of unproblematic social consensus. On what basis, then, can an evaluation or critique of the moral adequacy of an action be conducted? On the face of it, interpretation seems unlikely to provide an answer. To many, the conduct of interpretation connotes relativism, a subjective exegesis that operates only internally to the text and so abandons the possibility of genuine critique. But this characterization is unwarranted; we have already seen that interpretation considers both the narrative and its setting.

One way to appreciate the close interconnections of interpretation and evaluation is by reviewing the debate between Gadamer and Habermas on the relations between hermeneutics and critical theory (see McCarthy, 1978; Mendelson, 1979; Misgeld, 1976; Ormiston and Schrift, 1990; Ricoeur, 1990). Habermas's interest in hermeneutics was piqued by its emphasis on the essentially historical dimension of understanding and interpretation (Habermas, 1967). Gadamer (1985) argued that every analysis is structured by the analyst's interested position in a cultural tradition. This accorded well with the belief, central to critical theory, that any claim to have successfully adopted a neutral, detached, and objective attitude should be viewed as ideological. As McCarthy (1978, p. 179) puts it, Habermas came to see that "if the social scientist is not to proceed with his head in the sand, he must reflectively take into account the dependence of his conceptual apparatus on a prior understanding that is rooted in his own sociocultural situation. He must become hermeneutically and historically self-conscious."

This view gibed with Habermas's (1971) analysis of knowledge constitutive interests. But precisely because Gadamer insisted that the act of interpretation is shaped through and through by tradition, Habermas maintained that hermeneutic interpretation needs to be conjoined with a critique of ideology in order to question the tradition's legitimacy and authority. Tradition, in his view, contains elements of distortion, repression, and domination from which we must struggle to free ourselves. Rational reflection, a matter of distancing and critique rather than of interpretation, can profoundly alter the medium of tradition. Critical theory and hermeneutics could, in this sense, work as a team: "Hermeneutics comes up against the walls of the traditional framework from the inside, as it were. As soon as these boundaries have been experienced and recognized, cultural traditions can no longer be posed as absolute. . . . Hermeneutic experience that encounters this dependency of the symbolic framework on actual conditions changes into the critique of ideology" (Habermas, 1967, cited in McCarthy, 1978, p. 183). But this kind of critique requires a system of reference that is located outside or beyond tradition. Habermas sought this critical position in an analysis of economic and political forces operating, at a level distinct from that of language, to establish material conditions that provide an objective framework for social action.

Gadamer (1990) responded that Habermas presented a "dogmatic" conception of critique, and that reflection and critique themselves occupy a place in traditional practices. Furthermore, the operation of political and economic interests could, he argued, be brought to light in interpretation, as preconceptions and prejudgments. Reflection and understanding should not be viewed as distinct, even opposed, in the sense that one deals with critique and the other with interpretation. Reflection is an integral moment of struggling to understand, and, in addition, reflection is itself always partial and incomplete, based on preconceptions. At the same time, interpretation can break down any tradition's claim to be natural and objective.

It becomes clear in reviewing this debate that hermeneutics and critical theory are by no means radically at odds; on the contrary, they share presuppositions about knowledge and interest, tradition and understanding. Each places emphasis on elements tacit but present in the other. Both employ the strategy of assigning quasi-transcendental status to certain fundamental types of action (Mendelson, 1979); both see concerned engagement constructing apparently natural knowledge and artifacts. The Marxist tradition of critical theory employs interpretation and presupposes an existential analysis not at odds with Heidegger's account of the production of the person and the reproduction of society in and through praxis, including both labor and other forms of productive activity (for an analysis of Marx's "social ontology," see Gould, 1978; for Marx's phenomenological method, especially in the *Grundrisse* and *Capital*, see Ollman, 1990; Bologh, 1979). And hermeneutics, "radical hermeneutics" as Caputo (1987) has called it, entails a critique of appearances.

Reviewing this debate, Ricoeur (1990, p. 321) argues that although "the gesture of hermeneutics is a humble one of acknowledging the historical conditions to which all human understanding is subsumed in the reign of finitude; [while] that of the critique of ideology is a proud gesture of defiance directed against the distortions of human communication," the hermeneutics of texts nevertheless can provide a way to meet the demand for a critique of ideology. What makes such a critique possible is a dialectical tension between an experience of belonging and an alienating distancing, and this is found, Ricoeur suggests, precisely in textual interpretation. The fixing of narrative as text gives it the autonomy that we have already described, and a structure that is objective without being that of a natural object. In interpreting narrative text, we should never be content with a naive surface reading but instead should seek to articulate its structure through a critique of the means whereby its appearances are generated and maintained. Furthermore, when a narrative text "unfolds" a world of nonostensive reference, it makes possible a critique of the real world and, equally, of the illusions of the subject. All narratives, not just those we call fictional, entail a redescription, a creative mimesis, of the world we say is real. As such they point toward a new way of ordering the world.

In the opening vignette of this chapter, Ann's "telling" on her playmates evinces this characteristic of narrative. Her narration of events constitutes a call for action: the righting of a wrong; an intervention by the teacher to establish moral order. Ann describes a series of events so as to critique it. Hers is a tale of tragedy, albeit on a small and quotidian scale. Her narrative articulates a world where what *did* happen is not what *ought* to have happened. We can begin to articulate the world of the playground as she comprehends it (the "facts" and "values" that appear), as well as the concern with which she is engaged in that world (see Packer and Scott, 1991). Ann takes the practice of turn taking, and the requesting of turns, for granted. She grants Kathryn a certain authority while at the same time questioning the exercise of that authority. She calls upon the teacher's power to intervene and sanction, evincing a complex grasp of the intersecting ways of peers and adults at the preschool. We find that her narrative makes reference to a telos, a directedness, that organizes her activity also. We may find ourselves critical of that telos and the moral ordering that it implies; or we may find our eyes opened to heretofore unseen possibilities in the activity of young children.

The stories that people tell, then, press forward from the actual into the possible; they show how the world, and its people, could be different, could be better. People tell stories when their lives press forward against some blockage or breakdown. "Making sense" is seldom a casual exercise; we struggle to make sense in order to make our world different, to make ourselves different. In this activity lies a way of thinking of moral development not as the inevitable construction of universal ethical principles, but as the contingent, partial, and precarious attainment of a moral order, with both subjective and objective aspects, whose telos becomes apparent in the effort to make sense of, and overcome, practical problems of human relationships.

Conclusion

There is an illusory assumption in developmental psychology that contemporary children's development has escaped from tradition (or, more accurately, that tradition is simply irrelevant to it), that it is a matter of logical constructions derived only from relations in the present. But this idea of children individually constructing progressively advanced and elaborated schemes for instrumental mastery and social efficacy has to be understood historically, as a product of our modern world and the self-understanding it entails. In this world the ideology of the "rational system" predominates. The power, therefore, of giving fresh attention to narrative text stems, in part, from the example such texts provide of complex systems of internal relations, whose elements cannot be defined or described in isolation. This contrasts both with the image of purely external transactions between independent entities that drives statistical analysis, and with the image of the logical holism of a rational system emphasized by structural epistemologists and cognitive scientists. Both these images of the human world exclude all reference to its constitutive social and historical grounding, and to the interested stance of we who live in it.

We often take for granted our purposes when we study children's morality and moral development. Although it is easy to see ourselves as mature and those we study as somehow less formed, less informed, to think that we as adults are ahead of them, they are nonetheless our future, and in that regard their way lies ahead of ours. They will play out the possibilities they take from us, possibilities that we have handed down to them. We are their guardians now, but they will become guardians of our tradition and culture. If we can see, and understand, how they are taking up the ways we have been living, generally unreflectively, we are in a better position to understand how we live and evaluate what we are giving them. Their difficulties reflect our own problems and failures. An understanding of the conflicts that they work to resolve may enable us to change for the better the world in which we all live. The narratives that they construct and recount to their peers and to adults voice our conflicts and contradictions and point out new possibilities from which we all can learn.

References

Aristotle. *Rhetoric*. (W. Rhys Roberts, trans.) New York: Random House, 1954.

Berger, P. L., Berger, R., and Kellner, H. *The Homeless Mind: Modernization and Consciousness*. New York: Random House, 1973.

Blasi, A. "Moral Identity: Its Role in Moral Functioning." In W. Kurtines and J. Gewirtz (eds.), *Morality, Moral Behavior, and Moral Development*. New York: Wiley, 1984.

Bologh, R. W. *Dialectical Phenomenology: Marx's Method*. New York: Routledge & Kegan Paul, 1979.

Brown, L. M. "Moral Orientations and Epistemology: A Conceptual Analysis." Unpublished manuscript, Graduate School of Education, Harvard University, 1986.

Brown, L. M., Debold, E., Tappan, M. B., and Gilligan, C. "Reading Narratives of Conflict and Choice for Self and Moral Voice: A Relational Method." In W. Kurtines and J. Gewirtz (eds.), *Handbook of Moral Behavior and Development: Theory, Research, and Application*. Hillsdale, N.J.: Erlbaum, 1991.

Brown, L. M., Tappan, M. B., Gilligan, C., Miller, B., and Argyris, D. "Reading for Self and Moral Voice: A Method for Interpreting Narratives of Real-Life Moral Conflict and Choice." In M. J. Packer and R. Addison (eds.), *Entering the Circle: Hermeneutic Investigation in Psychology*. Albany: State University of New York Press, 1989.

Bruner, J. *Actual Minds, Possible Worlds*. Cambridge, Mass.: Harvard University Press, 1986.

Bruner, J. "Life as Narrative." *Social Research*, 1987, *54*, 11–32.

Caputo, J. *Radical Hermeneutics: Repetition, Deconstruction, and the Hermeneutic Project*. Bloomington: Indiana University Press, 1987.

De Rivera, J. "A Structural Theory of the Emotions." *Psychological Issues*, 1977, *10*, 1–178.

Dilthey, W. "The Development of Hermeneutics." In *Dilthey: Selected Writings*. (H. Rickman, ed. and trans.) Cambridge, England: Cambridge University Press, 1976. (Originally published 1900.)

Fish, S. *Doing What Comes Naturally: Change, Rhetoric, and the Practice of Theory in Literary and Legal Studies*. Durham, N.C.: Duke University Press, 1989.

Gadamer, H.-G. *Truth and Method*. New York: Crossroad, 1985. (Originally published 1960.)

Gadamer, H.-G. "The Universality of the Hermeneutic Problem." In G. Ormiston and A. Schrift (eds.), *The Hermeneutic Tradition: From Ast to Ricoeur*. Albany: State University of New York Press, 1990. (Originally published 1965.)

Gilligan, C. *In a Different Voice: Psychological Theory and Women's Development*. Cambridge, Mass.: Harvard University Press, 1982.

Gould, C. C. *Marx's Social Ontology: Individuality and Community in Marx's Theory of Social Relations*. Cambridge, Mass.: MIT Press, 1978.

Greimas, A., and Courtes, J. "The Cognitive Dimension of Narrative Discourse." *New Literary History*, 1976, *7*, 433–447.

Habermas, J. "Zur Logik der Sozialwissenschaften" [The logic of sociologies]. *Philosophische Rundschau* [Philosophy review], 1967, *5*, 174.

Habermas, J. *Knowledge and Human Interests*. (J. Shapiro, trans.) Boston: Beacon Press, 1971. (Originally published 1968.)

Hall, R., and Cobey, V. "Emotion as Transformation of the World." *Journal of Phenomenological Psychology*, 1976, *6*, 180–198.

Heidegger, M. *Being and Time*. (J. Macquarrie and E. Robinson, trans.) New York: Harper & Row, 1962. (Originally published 1927.)

Honey, M. "The Interview as Text: Hermeneutics Considered as a Model for Analyzing the Clinically Informed Research Interview." *Human Development,* 1987, *30,* 69–82.

Ingarden, R. *The Literary Work of Art.* Evanston, Ill.: Northwestern University Press, 1973.

Iser, W. *The Act of Reading: A Theory of Aesthetic Response.* Baltimore, Md.: Johns Hopkins University Press, 1978.

Jauss, H. *Aesthetic Experience and Literary Hermeneutics.* Minneapolis: University of Minnesota Press, 1977.

Jauss, H. *Toward an Aesthetic of Reception.* Minneapolis: University of Minnesota Press, 1982.

Jonsen, A. R., and Toulmin, S. *The Abuse of Casuistry: A History of Moral Reasoning.* Berkeley and Los Angeles: University of California Press, 1988.

Kohlberg, L. *Essays on Moral Development.* Vol. 1: *The Philosophy of Moral Development.* New York: Harper & Row, 1981.

Kohlberg, L. *Essays on Moral Development.* Vol. 2: *The Psychology of Moral Development.* New York: Harper & Row, 1984.

Kuhn, T. *The Structure of Scientific Revolutions.* (2nd ed.) Chicago: University of Chicago Press, 1970.

McCarthy, T. *The Critical Theory of Jürgen Habermas.* Cambridge, Mass.: MIT Press, 1978.

MacIntyre, A. *After Virtue: A Study in Moral Theory.* (2nd ed.) South Bend, Ind.: University of Notre Dame Press, 1984.

MacIntyre, A. *Whose Justice? Which Rationality?* South Bend, Ind.: University of Notre Dame Press, 1988.

Mendelson, J. "The Habermas-Gadamer Debate." *New German Critique,* 1979, *18,* 44–73.

Misgeld, D. "Critical Theory and Hermeneutics: The Debate Between Habermas and Gadamer." In J. O'Neill (ed.), *On Critical Theory.* New York: Seabury Press, 1976.

Mishler, E. *Research Interviewing: Context and Narrative.* Cambridge, Mass.: Harvard University Press, 1986.

Ollman, B. "Putting Dialectics to Work: The Process of Abstraction in Marx's Method." *Rethinking Marxism,* 1990, *3,* 26–74.

Ormiston, G., and Schrift, A. (eds.). *The Hermeneutic Tradition: From Ast to Ricoeur.* Albany: State University of New York Press, 1990.

Packer, M. J. "Hermeneutic Inquiry in the Study of Human Conduct." *American Psychologist,* 1985, *40,* 1081–1093.

Packer, M. J. "Tracing the Hermeneutic Circle: Articulating an Ontical Study of Moral Conflicts." In M. J. Packer and R. Addison (eds.), *Entering the Circle: Hermeneutic Investigation in Psychology.* Albany: State University of New York Press, 1989.

Packer, M. J., and Addison, R. "Evaluating an Interpretive Account." In M. J. Packer and R. Addison (eds.), *Entering the Circle: Hermeneutic Investigation in Psychology.* Albany: State University of New York Press, 1989.

Packer, M. J., and Richardson, E. "Analytic Hermeneutics and the Study of Morality in Action." In W. Kurtines and J. Gewirtz (eds.), *Handbook of Moral Behavior and Development: Theory, Research, and Application.* Hillsdale, N.J.: Erlbaum, 1991.

Packer, M. J., and Scott, B. "The Hermeneutic Investigation of Peer Relations." In L. T. Winegar and J. Valsiner (eds.), *Children's Development Within Social Contexts: Metatheoretical, Theoretical, and Methodological Issues.* Hillsdale, N.J.: Erlbaum, 1991.

Prince, G. *A Dictionary of Narratology.* Lincoln: University of Nebraska Press, 1987.

Propp, V. *Morphology of the Folktale*. (L. Scott, trans.) Austin: University of Texas Press, 1968.

Ricoeur, P. "Ethics and Culture: Habermas and Gadamer in Dialogue." *Philosophy Today*, 1973, *17*, 153–165.

Ricoeur, P. "The Model of the Text: Meaningful Action Considered as a Text." In P. Rabinow and W. Sullivan (eds.), *Interpretive Social Science: A Reader*. Berkeley and Los Angeles: University of California Press, 1979. (Originally published 1971.)

Ricoeur, P. *Time and Narrative*. Vol. 1. Chicago: University of Chicago Press, 1984.

Ricoeur, P. *Time and Narrative*. Vol. 2. Chicago: University of Chicago Press, 1985.

Ricoeur, P. *Time and Narrative*. Vol. 3. Chicago: University of Chicago Press, 1988.

Ricoeur, P. "Hermeneutics and the Critique of Ideology." In G. Ormiston and A. Schrift (eds.), *The Hermeneutic Tradition: From Ast to Ricoeur*. Albany: State University of New York Press, 1990. (Originally published 1973.)

Sarbin, T. (ed.). *Narrative Psychology: The Storied Nature of Human Conduct*. New York: Praeger, 1986.

Spence, D. *Narrative Truth and Historical Truth: Meaning and Interpretation in Psychoanalysis*. New York: Norton, 1982.

Suchman, L., and Jordan, B. "Interactional Troubles in Face-to-Face Survey Interviews." *Journal of the American Statistical Association*, 1990, *85*, 232–253.

Tappan, M. B. "Hermeneutics and Moral Development: Interpreting Narrative Representations of Moral Experience." *Developmental Review*, 1990, *10*, 239–265.

Tappan, M. B. "Texts and Contexts: Language, Culture, and the Development of Moral Functioning." In L. T. Winegar and J. Valsiner (eds.), *Children's Development Within Social Contexts: Metatheoretical, Theoretical, and Methodological Issues*. Hillsdale, N.J.: Erlbaum, 1991.

Taylor, C. *Sources of the Self: The Makings of the Modern Identity*. Cambridge, Mass.: Harvard University Press, 1989.

White, H. "The Value of Narrativity in the Representation of Reality." In W. Mitchell (ed.), *On Narrative*. Chicago: University of Chicago Press, 1981.

Martin J. Packer is assistant professor in the School of Education at the University of Michigan, Ann Arbor. His research interests include social development in peer relations, hermeneutic methods, and the phenomenology of everyday life.

The concept of development, whatever the specific domain of interest, is intrinsically bound up with both the idea of narrative and the idea of the moral.

Rewriting the Self:
Development as Moral Practice

Mark Freeman

In this chapter I develop the argument that the idea of narrative must be understood not only as a methodological approach to the study of moral development but also as an intrinsic facet of the concept of development. Further, and by extension, I argue that the concept of development, taken here in the broad sense of a progressive movement toward desired ends, is *necessarily* tied to the moral, for the simple reason that this progressive movement itself is unthinkable outside of some conception of where it *ought* to be heading. To this extent, it can plausibly be maintained that the concept of development, whatever the specific domain of interest, is intrinsically bound up with both the idea of narrative and the idea of the moral. With these brief introductory comments in mind, an important question immediately arises: If, in fact, there is no objectively based, universally prescribable "ought" to be identified a priori, that is, ahead of the dynamic movement of life itself, then how are we to speak about development at all?

Consider for a moment what two artists whom my colleagues and I studied have had to say about their own respective processes of "development." One of them, having carried out his work for a number of years under what he called "masklike" values, eventually realized that he had unwittingly placed more importance on his being acceptable as a certain

The case history information referred to in this chapter was gathered as part of a research project conducted at the University of Chicago, under the direction of Mihaly Csikszentmihalyi, Jacob W. Getzels, and Stephen P. Kahn, funded by the Spencer Foundation and the MacArthur Foundation.

kind of artist than on the work itself. "The kinds of things I had done, in large part," he admits, "were not based on my inner need or even personal goals so much as what I thought others wanted to see or what others thought was good, valuable." This concern with others' values changed, however, when his view of what his artistic activities were about became "far less important" than it had been in the past. Indeed, he went on to say, a concern for what is acceptable "is no longer even a question," for it simply does not matter what others think, at least not to a true artist. "Painting is fiction," he decided; "it hasn't got anything to do with truth. . . . Painting doesn't have to be fixed according to the rules of the world, the universe, the laws." It should be a creative outlet, a vehicle for discovery and play, a means to escape and perhaps critique "social and cultural confinements," nothing more. He was greatly relieved to have arrived at this realization, for he was finally able to look within, rather than without, and thus embody more fully what he believed to be the true aim of art.

A woman with whom we spoke had a quite different story to tell. In her own eyes, apparently, what was of critical importance was that she attend *more* to others than she had in the past. By virtue of her own fundamentally ruleless activities, which had culminated in a highly abstract, conceptual kind of art that was accessible only to the elite, she had managed to cut herself off from the people, a situation that she ultimately experienced as "hypocritical" and "disgusting." She therefore tried, consciously, to create works of art that would appeal to more than a select few; anyone off the street should be able to see what she was trying to do, she felt. The truth of the matter was, "Any artist, if they were totally honest, would say that they wanted everybody in the world to love what they did, to understand it." But it was precisely this communicative dimension of art that had been left behind in her own process of becoming a member in good standing of the artistic avant-garde. For this woman, then, the aim of art was not play, acceptability be damned; the aim was rather to speak to others so that their worlds might become enlarged.

There were numerous other developmental stories told as well in our research: An African-American artist, unable to afford the "luxury" of doing art for art's sake, felt the need to politically mobilize his community, even if this meant becoming marginal to the (white) art world; another artist gradually realized that art without some connection to the transcendent, however difficult this may be to define in the modern age, was empty and unreal; another artist, unable to continue locking himself away in a studio while the environment was being threatened with destruction, decided that art devoid of political ends was bankrupt and self-indulgent; and yet another, still convinced that art and politics were two entirely separate matters, finally managed to convince herself that art could indeed be important on its own terms and that, consequently, it was essential that artists not buy into a fundamentally utilitarian point of view. The stories go on.

What, then, are we to make of this vast proliferation of different voices, telling different stories, each of which is morally charged in its own unique way? And what, furthermore, are we to make of the fact that each of these different voices is telling a story that is explicitly about his or her own development, about what art ought to be and do? If we are to take these people on their own words, then it would appear that they have each developed in some way. At the same time, however, it should be amply clear that it is difficult, if not impossible, to identify some sort of generic set of criteria that applies to the lot of them. We thus return to the question posed earlier: How exactly are we to speak of the process of development in the absence of an a priori criteriological framework?

The Problem of Ends

In line with the view of development proposed by Piaget, Kohlberg, and other structural, normatively based theorists, the progressive movement of the self is predicated as a function of some form or other of a discrete end or telos. That is, normatively based theories of development, precisely by virtue of this very dimension of normativity, must necessarily posit an outcome to which the process of development is headed. In this respect, the idea of narrative is already relevant: It is only as a function of the designated end that we can speak of the developmental process that gives rise to it.

Now, in a distinct sense, it is exactly this problem of the ends of development that has served as a focal point for critiques of extant models, particularly Kohlberg's. If the ends prescribed by these models are indeed contestable, by virtue of their applying to certain groups of people—boys and men, for instance—more than to others, then so too is the process of development thought to culminate in them. Along these lines, Gilligan's (1982) well-known critique of Kohlberg's model may be described very broadly as a contestation about the ends of development as well as the process itself, the two mutually defining and constituting one another. Her argument was essentially that rather than posit a single line of development, it was preferable to posit two distinct developmental "voices," male and female, existing in a kind of counterpoint, which in turn serve to highlight the dialectical tension between justice and care.

This revision of the process of development, laudable though it may be, nevertheless leads one to ask much the same sorts of questions that were initially posed in regard to Kohlberg's model: Are the ends prescribed by Gilligan and other developmental revisionists definitive or are they, too, essentially contestable? More generally, although it may be possible within a specific cultural context to articulate ends possessing a fair degree of generality and extension across diverse groups of people, is it in fact possible to articulate ends that are somehow binding to and for entire groups of people—males and females, for instance? Or, to put the matter baldly, are the ends of development better left for individuals to decide?

Lest these questions sound both too relativistic and too individualistic, let me offer two qualifications. I am not claiming that there do not exist better and worse modes of being in the world, or that development is some sort of narcissistic free-for-all; every judgment we make and every course of action we adopt is thoroughly circumscribed by those conceptions of the good extant in a given culture. Stated another way, these conceptions, far from being merely detachable, here one day and gone the next, are part and parcel of our very existence as particular kinds of subjects inhabiting a certain social world, a certain discursive and practical order; they are wholly enmeshed with who and what we regard ourselves to be. But are we, as developmental psychologists, prepared to attempt that audacious leap into determining *the* good about which philosophers, theologians, and others have been battling for centuries?

Consider again for a moment the concept of development itself. What it presupposes, among other things, is something like a continuous and more-or-less unified subject, the trajectory of whose life can be traced in a continuous and more-or-less unified fashion. Now, not only is it the case that certain other cultures "refrain" from positing such a subject, but there are some people within the very ranks of our own modern Western culture who are also interested in doing so. The subject, it might be argued, is merely an effect of language, or an outdated legacy of humanism, or an imaginary artifact of "desire." As concerns the concept of development, therefore, the argument might continue, this is nothing more than a necessary correlate of precisely that illusion of a unified subjectivity that must be cast into question. As concerns the idea of narrative, finally, while many of us in the social sciences have found in this idea a new and challenging approach to the issues that concern us, it too may be seen as outdatedly humanistic: In presuming that the narratives people tell about themselves are anything other than (mere) fictions, constructed in line with the kinds of stories told in a given culture, it could very well be that we are deluding ourselves in supposing that they provide us any useful information at all.

Given these sorts of suspicions, as embodied particularly in certain strands of what is sometimes called "poststructuralist" thinking (see Smith, 1988, for an incisive review and critique; also Foucault, 1977, 1980), there is little doubt that were some of these "poststructuralists" to read the present volume, they might be utterly perplexed at the fact that some of us still insist on talking about the "self," "development," and "narrative." This may of course be their problem, not ours. My own inclination, in fact, is to think this is so. Nevertheless, the point is simply that there exists a whole host of contestable assumptions involved in what we are doing here—exemplified clearly by, among other things, the title of this volume—that it behooves us to acknowledge and avow, if only for the sake of knowing where we stand.

The second qualification, very much related to the first, has to do with the issue of individualism. As MacIntyre (1981) has argued, for instance, largely in response to some of the claims discussed above, it may be that a good portion of the suspicion and skepticism that we witness in contemporary discourse about the self, development, and so on is an effect not only of new-found philosophical insights about these notions but also of a social climate in which it has become progressively more difficult to articulate, with any sense of certainty and any degree of consensus, what the ends of human life might be. Even if "the language and appearances of morality persist," MacIntyre (1981, p. 5) notes, it is no less clear, to him at any rate, that "the integral substance of morality has to a large degree been fragmented and then in part destroyed." Tragically enough, he goes on to suggest, this fragmentation and destruction may be cause for celebration for some. The absence of a firmly rooted conception of a "whole human life," meaningful in its unity, "passes to some degree unnoticed" and is experienced "not as loss, but as self-congratulatory gain, as the emergence of the individual freed on the one hand from the social bonds of those constraining hierarchies which the modern world rejected at its birth and on the other hand from what modernity has taken to be the suspicions of teleology" (1981, p. 32). In any case, whatever value we may wish to place on the transition to which MacIntyre refers, it is evident that "the peculiarly modern self, the emotivist self, in acquiring sovereignty in its own realm lost its traditional boundaries provided by a social identity and a view of human life as ordered to a given end" (p. 32). In sum, then, MacIntyre seems to suggest that the essential contestability of developmental ends, far from merely being a philosophical insight into the ostensibly inescapable relativity of what is deemed moral, is itself a symptom of moral decay, the absence of a definable and defensible moral ground being made manifest in the form of relativistic moral epistemologies that magically transform our vertigo into a virtue.

Assuming there is some validity to what MacIntyre has to say in this context, there is a critical question that needs to be asked. If we have indeed managed to lose a view of human life "as ordered to a given end," as he suggests, does this mean that there is ultimately no rhyme or reason to the changes we undergo across the course of our lives? Stated another way, if in fact there is no universally binding end to which life is believed to lead, is the very concept of development "fragmented and then in part destroyed," the rational history of days gone by being replaced, in true nihilistic fashion, with a decidedly irrational one?

Narrative and Development

My own inclination is to answer the prior question with a cautious but firm no. That is, I am suggesting that even though the prescription of a "given end" may not be forthcoming, at least at this moment in history, it may still be possible to speak cogently about the process of development. But yet again, how? Here the idea of narrative comes to the forefront of our concerns. Instead of conceiving of development as a process that culminates in a given end, might it not be conceived as a process of reconstructing ends, of *rewriting* them (Freeman, in press; Freeman and Robinson, 1990), in line with the ever-changing tasks and moral demands of one's life?

There is an additional, more radical implication to be drawn from this point. To the extent that there exists a given end, whether formal operations, postconventional moral judgments, or what have you, it follows that the concept of development retains its traditional connotations of being fundamentally forward-looking; whatever transpires during the developmental process is headed *toward* that end. To the extent that there does not exist such a given end, however—indeed, to the extent that the multiplicity of possible ends are articulated *through* the developmental process itself, in line with the aforementioned tasks and moral demands of one's life—the trajectory of developmental transformation can only be told in *retrospect,* after one has arrived at a position from which to judge the preferability of who and what one has become over who and what one was. In other words, if in fact it is at all plausible to say that there exist *emergent* developmental ends, which, precisely by virtue of their emergence, render previous ends insufficient or inferior through their very juxtaposition against them, then development, rather than being seen as a teleologically driven push toward the future, is instead to be seen as a never-ending retrospective story of transformation.

Along these lines, we can never quite say where development is or ought to be headed, not ahead of time at any rate; we can only say where it has been. And it is for this reason, above all others, that we might see in the idea of narrative both an appropriate methodological tool for studying development as well as an appropriate theoretical lens for conceptualizing it (Freeman, 1984; Tappan, 1989): The histories that people tell, of the contradictions and dilemmas that have given rise to what can arguably be deemed "better" modes of knowing and being, translate into a vision of development predicated on the, in principle, ceaseless reconstruction of ends.

Of course, it might be argued that there is something decidedly tragic about this view of development. If the reconstruction of the ends of life is in itself endless, then one can never be sure about the ultimate validity of where one is now; there will always exist the possibility that one's most deeply felt moral certainties will explode in the future. Furthermore, perhaps for some it will be difficult to reconcile the idea of living a life that is not necessarily leading to anywhere in particular; in true existential fashion, there might be a measure of anguish attendant to the realization that there will never be, that there *can* never be, a final resting place, where one shuts the door, so to speak, on the travails of the past, only to gaze back at them in relief that they are gone forever. Again, with no absolute end in sight, one will undoubtedly realize that there will be travails to come, which, in turn, will signal the fact that a measure of developmental "humility" will always be called for: No matter how certain one is that he or she has finally found the true way, this certainty will inevitably have to be tempered by the knowledge that one has more than likely felt this way before, even repeatedly perhaps, only to see this very certainty cast into question by the emergence of new developmental challenges and their resultant ends. For those with a serious hankering for the absolute, therefore, the view of development being espoused here might sound a bit too much like the Nietzschean proclamation that God is dead.

But there is another way entirely of looking at these matters. Let me, then, enumerate several reasons for why this view of development might offer a useful and positive alternative to extant models.

Development in Context

First, if there is no absolute end or ceiling to the process of development, then we are able to clear a space for the pragmatically desirable possibility that it is a potentially lifelong process. As Robinson and I have argued elsewhere (Freeman and Robinson, 1990), the very question of whether there is something like development in adulthood and old age, for instance, is somewhat damaging, particularly for those whose developmental fates are at stake: Depending on what we, as developmental researchers and theorists, decide development is, they may or may not be seen as capable of it. Children obviously develop, we might argue; for adulthood and beyond it is unclear. But what can this possibly mean? Are we about to proffer the allegedly empirically based conclusion that there may not *be* development in old age and thus prevent people from even entertaining the possibility that there is more room for them to grow as human beings?

The question at hand can only be raised from the perspective of a structural, normatively based theoretical model that posits some form or another of a possible ceiling. But it could very well be that this sort of theoretical model blinds us to the possibility of the kind of psychological growth of which I have just spoken; the model presumes that development is either a natural or quasi-natural process, the growth and decay of human beings being conceived essentially on the analogy of organic bodies, whether animals or plants. I am not about to contend that we do not have these bodies, nor am I about to contend that they do not decay. But isn't even the most frail and wizened among us sometimes able to move forward as a human being, to a place that is arguably better than where he or she was?

This is not merely an academic point. It could certainly be argued that there are many people, in our own culture especially, who become convinced that once their days are numbered, there is little left to do but live them out stoically; since they "know" that aging means decline, they may assent, even if unwittingly, to the cultural prescription. The implication is important: It would appear that there is a connection, however indirect, between the theoretical models presently in existence and the psychological experience of aging itself. Might it not be said, therefore, that models of development, in addition to *representing* people, *constitute* them as people of a particular sort? If so, then it behooves us to think about development in a different way, if only to explore those uncharted regions of human life that might have been given short shrift in our desire to delineate *the* end or ends of the process in question. In short, if there is any reason at all to suppose that human development can transpire as long as there is sentient life—which is to say that it is a potentially *infinite* process—then we ought to consider theoretical perspectives able to accommodate this supposition.

Second, the view of development offered here, by relying on the unique experiences that individuals recollect in telling the stories of their lives, clears a path toward acknowledging the multiplicity of ways that human beings might be said to develop. Development is not only able to transpire indefinitely from this perspective, then, but in an infinite number of different ways, depending on the persons in question, their respective sociocultural contexts, and so forth. To risk a bit of hackneyed postmodernism about why this diversity is to be considered a desirable thing, suffice it to say that living in the world we do, it would seem to be wise to see amidst the different lives that people lead alternatives to our own. In raising the possibility that other people in other sociocultural contexts might develop in entirely different ways than we do, in other words, we are given an opportunity for both other-critique and self-critique that we simply may not have had otherwise. Could it be, we may occasionally wish to ask, that we can sometimes become so thoroughly convinced of the validity of our own emergent developmental ends, ephemeral though they may be, that we fail to accommodate adequately the otherness of those we study, that we fail to see the possible validity of their emergent ends in relation to the contexts in which they live? If so, this failure is damaging not only to them, by virtue of our unwitting negation of who and what they might aspire to be, but also to us. For in negating the other, we deprive ourselves of just that dimension of dialogue, of different voices, that sometimes leads us to loosen some of our own solidified ways.

Third, and extending the point just discussed, it seems clear enough that by focusing on the multiplicity of different ways that people might be said to develop, in line with the different sociocultural contexts in which they live, we may place ourselves in a position to more fully acknowledge the social nature of development. Note that development has not always been seen in these terms. According to Weintraub (1975, 1978), for instance, there is good reason to believe that the path of development was formerly seen as carved out essential irrespective of social factors, the shape of one's life being seen as "unfolding" just the same no matter what the specific circumstances. Later in the course of history, however, with the emergence of what he calls "historical consciousness," we came to understand that there really was no separation of the wholly individual from the wholly social; the shape of one's life, therefore, was as much the product of social circumstances, accidents, and so forth as it was of one's own inchoate developmental potentiality.

The point is that the sociocultural contexts in which people live do not merely affect the course of development but also constitute and define it: The course of development, insofar as it takes place within the confines of language, convention, and so forth, assumes its specific shape as a function of the modes of discourse and social practice inherent to any given locale. A disclaimer is in order at this point. To say that individual development is constituted through sociocultural context is emphatically not to claim that development is *nothing but* a mere shadow of social reality, in the sense of being fundamentally epiphenomenal. Rather, all that is being claimed is that the forms that development assumes rely thoroughly on the contexts in which they take place: on some form or another of a "tradition" (see Gadamer, 1985, 1979) within which possibilities for speaking and thinking and acting are circumscribed.

Why, though, aside from the alleged theoretical importance of context, might it be useful to see development as socioculturally constituted? There are at least two reasons. First, to the extent that we explore developmental differences with reference to their respective real-life contexts rather than to some theoretically pregiven "metacontext," we are that much more likely to become attuned to those modes of development that are appropriate in a given locale. By exploring development within the context of some specific tradition, in other words, we are that much more likely to be respectful not only of what people are saying but also of what ends they deem optimal given the conditions of their lives. In this sense, of course, we might better hear in the proliferation of different developmental voices the possibility for dialogue and for arriving at a more expansive, comprehensive, and inclusive conception of what development can mean.

Second, and to me the more important reason for seeing development as socioculturally constituted, it is only with this viewpoint that we have in hand both a theoretical and a practical vehicle for considering the occasional necessity of sociocultural *change*. If, for instance, one's developmental possibilities are effectively cut short by the conditions obtaining in a given locale, might it not be useful to rethink these conditions and to consider ways in which they might be transformed so as to restart the process? We can frame this another way. If development has anything to do with new meanings being given to experience, and if these meanings are inseparable from language, and if, finally, language is part and parcel of the sociocultural world, then development ultimately has to do with negotiating both language and context and becoming cognizant of how they mediate one's experience. It is, in short, to claim *authority* for one's beliefs and actions, which is the most fundamental precondition for fashioning new forms of language and envisioning new contexts within which the developmental process can be continued (see Tappan, 1991, this volume).

Bakhtin (1986, p. 138) expressed the matter well: "The better a person understands the degree to which he is externally determined, the closer he comes to understanding and exercising his real freedom." This in itself is a process of rewriting: The artist who realized that his artistic activities were less a function of his own directives than those of others, for instance, had rewritten the meaning not only of those activities but also of his very self; only then did he acquire the freedom to think anew about who he was and what he might do in the future to create an environment more conducive to his own true interests and desires. Alongside *freedom,* therefore, there also arose, as a matter of course, a sense of *responsibility:* He would now be in the position to determine a suitable course of action.

In speaking about the "new" in what has been discussed above, I am by no means speaking of the *wholly* new, in the sense of the ex nihilo fashioning of language; "something created," Bakhtin (1986, p. 120) writes, "is always created out of something given (language, an observed phenomenon of reality, and experienced feeling, the speaking subject himself, something finalized in his world view, and so forth)." To this extent, development is inevitably circumscribed by the parameters of discourse extant in a given context; there is just so much one is able to say and do in a particular time and place. At the same time, though, "what is given," Bakhtin adds, "is completely transformed in what is created" (p. 120), which is precisely what allows us to see in the process of development a vehicle for both exposing the status quo of language and context and moving beyond it. "The task," in short, "consists in forcing the *thinglike* environment, which mechanically influences the personality, to begin to speak, that is, to reveal in it the potential word and tone, to transform it into a semantic context for the thinking, speaking, and acting (as well as creating) personality" (p. 164): Only then is development possible.

But how is this task to be realized? More specifically, how does one go about locating those new forms of language that might serve to move the process of development forward? The only way, I suggest, is in and through dialogue with others and with ourselves. This brings me to the fourth reason for considering the present perspective on development. By opening up the very concept of development in the manner described thus far, such that no single, absolute end is to be privileged ahead of time over any other, we also open up the possibility for dialogue, precisely about the infinitely multiple ends to which life might lead. Bakhtin's (1986, p. 7) comments are useful once again: "A meaning can only reveal its depths once it has encountered and come in contact with another, foreign meaning: they engage in a kind of dialogue, which surmounts the closedness and one-sidedness of these particular meanings."

What this implies, in turn, is that we, as people and as developmental psychologists, can serve not merely as faceless witnesses to the development or nondevelopment of those we study but also as partners in dialogue about the possible ends of life, able to engage voices that might otherwise have gone unheard.

Our problems, however, are far from over. Dialogue is all well and good, MacIntyre (1981) might say, but only if it is headed somewhere meaningful and important, namely, in the direction of some form of a given end. Perhaps, he would add, this notion of dialogue itself, laudable though it may seem on the surface, is testimony to the crisis we face: "The interminable and unsettlable character of so much contemporary moral debate arises from the heterogeneous and incommensurable concepts which inform the major premises from which the protagonists in such debates argue" (1981, p. 210). It arises, that is, out of an absence and a loss, out of just that moral abyss that cannot help but culminate in ceaseless chatter of the sort we see today, in developmental psychology and elsewhere. Is it possible to see in this alleged abyss any room for human beings to truly develop? Or are we seeing instead only "mock development," a simulation of the real thing, wrought out of the latest arbitrary fashions?

Genealogy, Narrative, and the Possibility of Human Progress

According to MacIntyre (1981; see also Bellah, Madsen, Sullivan, Swidler, and Tipton, 1985), there is a sense in which charting the trajectory of a human life has come to amount to little more than what Foucault (1980, p. 117), in the wake of Nietzsche, has called genealogy: "a form of history which can account for the constitution of knowledges, discourses, domains of objects, etc., without having to make reference to a subject which is either transcendental in relation to the field of events or runs in its empty sameness throughout the course of history." "Genealogy," Foucault (1977, p. 139) writes elsewhere, is thus "gray, meticulous, and patiently documentary"; it does not

> pretend to go back in time to restore an unbroken continuity that operates beyond the dispersion of forgotten things; its duty is not to demonstrate that the past actively exists in the present, that it continues secretly to animate the present, having imposed a predetermined form to all its vicissitudes. . . . On the contrary, to follow the complex course of descent [of a society or of a person] is to maintain passing events in their proper dispersion; it is to identify the accidents, the minute deviations—or, conversely, the complete reversals—the errors, the false ap-

praisals, and the faulty calculations that gave birth to those things that
continue to exist and have value for us; it is to discover that truth or
being do not lie at the root of what we know and what we are, but the
exteriority of accidents [p. 146].

Along these lines, then, the more traditional narrative history, that
continuous story of the order of the past, is nothing more than an illusory
continuity foisted upon the flux; and development, by extension, nothing
more than a second-order illusion, that of human progress, foisted upon
this alleged continuity. We would be wise, therefore, Foucault implies, to
undo these illusions by destroying this wished-for order. Genealogy thus
"disturbs what was previously considered immobile; it fragments what was
thought unified; it shows the heterogeneity of what was imagined consistent
with itself" (Foucault, 1977, p. 147). Again, it is true enough: "We want historians," and perhaps also developmental psychologists, "to confirm our
belief that the present rests upon profound intentions and immutable necessities. But the true historical sense confirms our existence among countless
lost events, without a landmark or a point of reference" (1977, p. 155).
Little wonder that MacIntyre and company are somewhat disturbed at this
sort of talk. And little wonder as well that they find in this historiographical
turnabout signs of the profound decay of moral life: The explosion of the
idea that life is to be conceived as ordered to a given end implies that the
best we can do is chart the accidents that compose it.

But why must it be presumed that if life is not teleologically ordered, if
it does not embody "immutable necessities," it is ultimately accidental and
irrational? The reason is that we still remain so committed, even if uncon-
sciously, to a decontextualized, dehistoricized view of the development of
the self that once context is admitted into the picture as an important
"variable," it becomes terrifically difficult to find an appropriate way to
speak about the matters at hand. More to the point, if in fact the ways that
human beings change over time is as variable and multiplicitous as the
contexts in which they live and, more specifically, the forms of language
they employ, why should we conclude that they are *developing* at all? Why
should we assume that they are doing anything more than *changing,* in line
with the different voices that they hear and internalize over the course of
time? More seriously still, and in line with the challenge posed by Foucault
and others, why should we assume that there is in fact a unified subject
who either develops *or* changes? Perhaps all that can be said is that different words emerge from roughly the same body over the course of time.

To say something as deceptively simple as "*a child develops morally*"
implies at least three serious and, for some, contestable assumptions: that
we can speak of *a* child who is a continuous and unified entity of some
sort; that this entity not only changes over time but does so in what can
arguably be deemed a progressive way; and that there is indeed a realm of

phenomena that can justifiably be called "moral." Let us deal briefly with each of these issues to see if we can arrive at a suitable way of responding to each.

While it is no doubt impossible to establish in any definitive way the existence of a continuous self (which is exactly why those of a positivist bent tend to question it), it seems to me that there is sufficient reason to posit it. The very emergence of language, which serves to name not only the world but the subject who beholds it, would appear to attest the existence of a continuous self. Yet, there is a challenge even here. According to Barthes (1977, p. 145), for instance, in his reflections on the idea of the author, "*I is nothing other than the instance saying I*"; the positing of a continuous self, therefore, is simply an extrapolation, originating in language. From his perspective, then, the emergence of language, rather than resulting in a self, merely results in the *idea* of a self; it is thus a fictional construct, having little more basis in reality than have the words that speak of it.

Are there any other "data" we might seize upon to bolster our belief in this elusive entity? I would say that there are. In addition to language, what makes for the continuity of the self is nothing other than those *narratives* we tell about ourselves—whether implicitly, in the course of reflection, or explicitly, in the course of speaking and writing—in order to account for who and what we are and how we might have gotten to be that way. Now, it is true that in conferring such important status on the idea of narrative, which is inseparably tied to language, we are admitting that the specific selves that we become are in large measure a function of the words we speak. But this does not necessarily mean that the self is a mere extrapolation or epiphenomenon or fiction; it only means that language is in large measure constitutive of selfhood, just as it is in large measure constitutive of everything else. We could claim, if we wished, that reality is also an extrapolation or epiphenomenon or fiction, and perhaps there are some who are inclined to do just that. But, to my mind, there is little reason to claim that the linguistic constitution of reality and of selfhood entails the further supposition that these things are ultimately illusions. The point here is that this elusive entity we call the self—in the modern, Western world at least (see Baumeister, 1987; Geertz, 1979; Mauss, 1979; Sampson, 1989; Shweder and Bourne, 1984; Weintraub, 1975; for relevant discussions)—assumes its specific form in and through narrative, that is, in and through the story of its genesis.

For the sake of moving on, therefore, let us assume that we can indeed speak of a more or less continuous self, and that it is all right to consider the next contestable assumption, that of development. I have just spoken of the story of the self's genesis. But again, how exactly do we make the leap from *story*, which can only be predicated in retrospect, to *development*, with its customary prospective orientation? Or, stated another way, why should we see in the succession of stories that people tell about themselves anything but just that—stories? The reason is that the stories that people tell about themselves, particularly when they are asked explicitly how they see themselves to have changed in the context of some domain of experience over time, are often not only about discrete behaviors—"I used to behave that way, now I behave this way"—but also about the reconstructed *meaning(s)* of their experience. When a group of adolescents interviewed some years ago (Freeman, Csikszentmihalyi, and Larson, 1986) were asked to recount changes they had undergone in their relations with family, with friends, and alone, for instance, they detailed some of their new-found realizations about what it meant to *be* a family member, with real-life people for parents; about what it meant to have friends, who were progressively being chosen for their authentic compatibility rather than for who they were in the eyes of others; about what it meant to spend time in solitude, reflectively, away from the confusing demands of others. Did they develop? The answer to me was an obvious yes, because what they had done was create *what they saw to be,* indeed *what they argued to be,* a new, more comprehensive and inclusive interpretive context within which to place their experience (see also Tappan, 1989).

Their situations would no doubt change as they grew older. Perhaps some of them would turn against their parents in the interest of furthering their own freedom. Perhaps authentic compatibility would later be judged of secondary importance to complementarity. Perhaps time alone would be regarded as too conducive to narcissistic preoccupation with one's self-worth, and there would be a decision instead to just live rather than analyze. And, in principle, as noted earlier, these rewritings could go on forever, in line with the individuals' ever-changing experiences, which would require new interpretive contexts once again to make sense of what was going on in their lives. Foucault is therefore quite right: Accidents do happen, and a significant portion of our lives has to do with responding to them in ways that are deemed appropriate. Furthermore, we often make some serious and, in retrospect, dreadful mistakes in terms of the interpretive contexts that we create in order to further our own understanding. At the very least, we can often see the patent inadequacy about the way we thought about or handled such and such a situation, the result being that we sometimes look back on our pasts with a profound sense of humility concerning the ignorant and inferior creatures we were: "How dumb," "How naive," "How immature," "How hasty," "How selfish," "How unselfish," and so on. But there is also no small measure of comfort to be derived from these frequently harsh realizations: We are no longer there; we are elsewhere; and the place at which we have arrived can arguably be judged to be a better one, if only for the time being.

But why "better"? This place of which I have just spoken could simply be different sometimes; we get a new angle on ourselves, see things in a different light than we had previously. But interpretations can surely be better as well. How do we know this? We know this precisely by the juxtaposition of our newly fashioned interpretive context against our old one, which becomes exposed as inadequate in the very process of its supersession. "The 'former' prejudice is not simply cast aside," Gadamer (1979, p. 157) writes, "whatever replaced it cannot present its credentials until the position under assault is itself unmasked and denounced as prejudice." And thus, "every 'new' position which replaces another continues to need the 'former' because it cannot itself be explained so long as it knows neither *in* what nor *by* what it is opposed" (p. 157).

The notion of better, of developmental *progress,* therefore, derives not from a comparison of two readings of experience held apart from one another in putatively objective fashion, but rather from their relationship, from the transformation of one into the other. "Now," one might say, "I have a more adequate understanding of this phenomenon before me." This, too, will no doubt change, and our humility, perhaps even our humiliation, will return once more. But we ought not to chide ourselves too much for our former foibles, for our own experiential world will in all likelihood have changed in the interim. Should we ever kick ourselves for our former foibles? Of course, but only if there is good reason to believe that our former interpretive contexts were inadequate given the situation we were in at the time.

At least one further problem arises here. Even though we may be thoroughly assured that the new interpretive stance we are taking toward the world is better than the old one, it is surely possible that we are deluding ourselves in believing this to be so; defenses and the like can undoubtedly enter into even the most sober and reasoned modes of judgment, moral and otherwise. How do we know, then, that we have experienced "true" development rather than "mock" development? What we need to do—and this advice is surely reminiscent of Freud, among others—is take our new interpretive stance out into the world and, rather than rest comfortably with it, see how well it coheres with that world. We need, in other words, to test it in relation to the experiences that we have and see if it is able to make more adequate sense of things than had previously been possible. If it is so able, then perhaps we were on to something. If not, then perhaps we had better think through our developmental options a bit more thoroughly. In any case, development, along the lines being drawn here, may be seen quite broadly as an effort at rewriting, via the establishment of a new interpretive context, some specific domain of experience and, simultaneously, the self: For in the very midst of rendering more adequate my view of such and such a domain of experience, I change as well, this new "text" before me being appropriated into the fabric of the self.

The Moral of the Story

It is difficult to tell a story, whether of oneself or another, without there being a moral component in it. Indeed, the very manner in which the story is told, its mode of "emplotment" (White, 1978), implies a moral stance; one has made a narrative choice, to tell this sort of story rather than that, and this choice often issues from the most fundamental beliefs, values, and ideals that one holds. In narratives concerning the development of the self, of course, such as those mentioned in conjunction with the artists discussed earlier, this moral component is even more obvious, for the simple reason that the very concept of development—inescapably tied as it is to what is colloquially called the *good*—cannot be thought apart from some conception of what ought to be. What this means, in turn, is that narratives of development, whatever the domain of experience being considered, are always and inevitably shot through with the moral, taken here in the very broad sense of predicating the existence of more and less preferable modes of being and knowing. Technical mastery aside, one cannot talk about artistic development, therefore, without making a moral claim about what art ought to be: It ought to be for the sake of free play, it ought to be for the sake of communication, it ought to be for the sake of raising political consciousness, and so on. The notion of what is preferable is thus inescapable.

But it is also a thorny notion with which to grapple. For some, MacIntyre perhaps, it may reek all too strongly of just that emotivist self that litters the landscape of modernity, with its ill-founded, idiosyncratic, rootless, and rudderless choices about who and what to be. Indeed, perhaps he would even argue, in response to the dialogical project of studying development outlined earlier, that what we are most likely to hear is a cacophony of monadic voices, each staking its own claims to that essentially empty conception of the good most in line with the desires of the moment. We do have a problem here. Short of some philosophico-moral breakthrough that allows us finally to bask in happy agreement about what *the* good is, we are indeed bound to hear lots of different voices, even within the confines of our own selves. But must this heterogeneous chorus of moral voices result in cacophony? Only to the extent that dialogue, with oneself and with others, is missing.

Now, I am not so idealistically sanguine about the road to the future as to suppose that there exists some communicative oasis where we all arrive; perhaps there will never be the wholesale erasure of competing claims about the good. But this inability to attain consensus is hardly to be seen as a necessary liability. Quite the contrary: It is only with competing claims on the table that dialogue—and development—is even possible, for it is only through juxtaposition and contradiction, between different modes of knowing and being, that one may be incited to move forward.

Yet, perhaps there still remains reason to be skeptical about this idea that dialogue about the good leads anywhere worthwhile. Dialogue, as we all know, can easily lead to argument, and argument to violence. For all we know, then, it could be that if all the artists discussed earlier were placed in a room to engage in dialogue about what it might mean to develop artistically, there would be a full-scale brawl. But if one is asked whether it is possible to imagine that there would be more salutary outcomes to this dialogue than there would be without it, it seems to me that the answer is clear enough. At the very least, perhaps it would be possible for some to acquire a healthy respect for what others are doing and to understand and appreciate more fully that there are other ways of carrying out a life than one's own.

In calling attention to the importance of dialogue about the good, I have made a moral choice: To speak with others about the good, I believe, is preferable to not doing so. I avow my own prejudices in setting forth my ideas. There can even be dialogue, of course, about the desirability of dialogue. Again, maybe for some there is entirely too much interminable moral chatter nowadays, and it is high time to lay down the law: When in doubt, they might say, turn to a regime; only then will the turbulence die down. It is alongside the moral fragmentation of which MacIntyre and others have spoken that we also see a wide variety of fundamentalisms, ranging from the religious to the intellectual; whatever will suffice to stop the rot.

There is another way entirely, however, of understanding our present situation. It could very well be that dialogue of the sort proposed here, rather than being seen as interminable and thus leading essentially nowhere, may instead be seen as a vehicle for making conscious certain aspects of moral life that might otherwise remain unconscious and unspoken: for moving us, in other words, from blind faith to true morality, however we may choose to define it. Dialogue, then, rather than being an end, is perhaps better understood as a beginning, which may lead us to a surer and more fully articulated sense of where we stand as moral beings.

Conclusion

The argument developed in this chapter is that the idea of narrative, rather than being seen only as a methodological approach to the study of development, is itself intrinsic to the process of development. What this means, in turn, is that in a distinct sense development is a fundamentally *retrospective* concept, predicated on what has been here called rewriting the self: It is only after one has arrived at what is arguably or demonstrably a better psychological place than where one has been before that development can be said to have occurred. By no means should this be taken to imply that narratives of development are merely fictions foisted upon what some might regard as the chaotic flux of life. Indeed, as has been suggested in previous chapters of this volume, life itself is always and inevitably mediated by narrative as well, which is what allows us to think and act in meaningful ways. In considering narratives of development, therefore, the interest is in showing precisely how meanings are renegotiated, refigured, and reauthorized, toward the end of constructing a new self who, through dialogue with and juxtaposition to the old, has articulated a better way.

We run into difficulties with this perspective, of course, when we recognize that one person's "better way" may not be deemed so by others, including ourselves. It could be, for instance, that upon seeing that an informant is simply mouthing the words of others and stopping short of authorizing his or her own language (Tappan, this volume), we will wish to act as midwives, assisting in the birth of new meaning; we will help these people find their own voices, amidst the welter of others. But what should be done when our informants' visions of development fly in the face of our own values, beliefs, and ideals? Isn't it the case that even when one has moved in the direction of truly claiming authority for one's life, there still exists the possibility that the new self that has been constructed will be, by basic standards of human decency, thoroughly objectionable? What if, for instance, our informants' developing capacity to claim authority for their beliefs and actions leads them to become authoritarian, in the ugliest sense of the word?

Even if in modernity's wake we cannot identify in absolute terms the ends of human development, it would nonetheless seem imperative for psychologists not only to be good, receptive, and undogmatic partners in dialogue but also to carry out these dialogues armed with a principle that I call, quite simply, *hope*: hope that we may succeed in furthering dialogue when the prospects of doing so seem dim, and hope that the authority people claim for themselves will be at least minimally in the service of such notable virtues as understanding, care, and compassion. In addition to abiding by those whom we study, therefore, we need to abide by ourselves, making sure that our own moral commitments are not wholly effaced in the interest of remaining neutral. Needless to say, the aim here is not to convince, which would be authoritarian in its own right, but to engage, with the hope that the ensuing dialogue will be open and real. Anything less would be an act of bad faith; it would be to abdicate our own sense of responsibility to ourselves and to others. If we are truly to be partners in dialogue, then, rather than faceless witnesses, we had better be prepared to dive into the fray every now and then. There are times when this is the only *moral* thing to do.

References

Bakhtin, M. M. *Speech Genres and Other Late Essays*. (V. McGee, trans.) Austin: University of Texas Press, 1986.

Barthes, R. *Image, Music, Text*. New York: Hill and Wang, 1977.

Baumeister, R. "How the Self Became a Problem: A Psychological Review of Historical Research." *Journal of Personality and Social Psychology*, 1987, 52 (1), 163–176.

Bellah, R. N., Madsen, R., Sullivan, W. M., Swidler, A., and Tipton, S. M. *Habits of the Heart: Individualism and Commitment in American Life*. Berkeley and Los Angeles: University of California Press, 1985.

Foucault, M. *Language, Counter-Memory, Practice*. Ithaca, N.Y.: Cornell University Press, 1977.

Foucault, M. *Power/Knowledge*. New York: Pantheon, 1980.

Freeman, M. "History, Narrative, and Life-Span Developmental Knowledge." *Human Development*, 1984, 27 (1), 1–19.

Freeman, M. *Rewriting the Self: History, Memory, Narrative*. New York: Routledge & Kegan Paul, in press.

Freeman, M., Csikszentmihalyi, M., and Larson, R. "Adolescence and Its Recollection: Toward an Interpretive Model of Development." *Merrill-Palmer Quarterly*, 1986, 32 (2), 167–185.

Freeman, M., and Robinson, R. "The Development Within: An Alternative Approach to the Study of Lives." *New Ideas in Psychology*, 1990, 8 (1), 53–72.

Gadamer, H.-G. "The Problem of Historical Consciousness." In P. Rabinow and W. M. Sullivan (eds.), *Interpretive Social Science: A Reader*. Berkeley and Los Angeles: University of California Press, 1979.

Gadamer, H.-G. *Truth and Method*. New York: Crossroad, 1985. (Originally published 1960.)

Geertz, C. "From the Native's Point of View: On the Nature of Anthropological Understanding." In P. Rabinow and W. Sullivan (eds.), *Interpretive Social Science: A Reader*. Berkeley and Los Angeles: University of California Press, 1979.

Gilligan, C. *In a Different Voice: Psychological Theory and Women's Development*. Cambridge, Mass.: Harvard University Press, 1982.

MacIntyre, A. *After Virtue: A Study in Moral Theory*. South Bend, Ind.: University of Notre Dame Press, 1981.

Mauss, M. *Essays in Sociology and Psychology*. New York: Routledge & Kegan Paul, 1979. (Originally published 1938.)

Sampson, E. "The Deconstruction of the Self." In J. Shotter and K. Gergen (eds.), *Texts of Identity*. Newbury Park, Calif.: Sage, 1989.

Shweder, R., and Bourne, E. "Does the Concept of the Person Vary Cross-Culturally?" In R. Shweder and R. LeVine (eds.), *Culture Theory: Essays on Mind, Self, and Emotion*. Cambridge, England: Cambridge University Press, 1984.

Smith, P. *Discerning the Subject*. Minneapolis: University of Minnesota Press, 1988.

Tappan, M. "Stories Lived and Stories Told: The Narrative Structure of Late Adolescent Moral Development." *Human Development*, 1989, 32 (5), 300–315.

Tappan, M. "Texts and Contexts: Language, Culture, and the Development of Moral Functioning." In L. T. Winegar and J. Valsiner (eds.), *Children's Development Within Social Contexts: Metatheoretical, Theoretical, and Methodological Issues*. Hillsdale, N.J.: Erlbaum, 1991.

Weintraub, K. "Autobiography and Historical Consciousness." *Critical Inquiry*, 1975, 1 (4), 821–848.

Weintraub, K. *The Value of the Individual: Self and Circumstance in Autobiography*. Chicago: University of Chicago Press, 1978.

White, H. *Tropics of Discourse*. Baltimore, Md.: Johns Hopkins University Press, 1978.

Mark Freeman is assistant professor of psychology at the College of the Holy Cross, Worcester, Massachusetts. He has written articles for such journals as Human Development, Psychoanalysis and Contemporary Thought, *and* New Ideas in Psychology *and is the author of the forthcoming* Rewriting the Self: History, Memory, Narrative, *to be published by Routledge & Kegan Paul.*

INDEX

ORDERING INFORMATION

NEW DIRECTIONS FOR CHILD DEVELOPMENT is a series of paperback books that presents the latest research findings on all aspects of children's psychological development, including their cognitive, social, moral, and emotional growth. Books in the series are published quarterly in Fall, Winter, Spring, and Summer and are available for purchase by subscription as well as by single copy.

SUBSCRIPTIONS for 1991 cost $52.00 for individuals (a savings of 20 percent over single-copy prices) and $70.00 for institutions, agencies, and libraries. Please do not send institutional checks for personal subscriptions. Standing orders are accepted.

SINGLE COPIES cost $17.95 when payment accompanies order. (California, New Jersey, New York, and Washington, D.C., residents please include appropriate sales tax.) Billed orders will be charged postage and handling.

DISCOUNTS FOR QUANTITY ORDERS are available. Please write to the address below for information.

ALL ORDERS must include either the name of an individual or an official purchase order number. Please submit your order as follows:
  Subscriptions: specify series and year subscription is to begin
  Single copies: include individual title code (such as CD1)

MAIL ALL ORDERS TO:
  Jossey-Bass Inc., Publishers
  350 Sansome Street
  San Francisco, California 94104

FOR SALES OUTSIDE OF THE UNITED STATES CONTACT:
  Maxwell Macmillan International Publishing Group
  866 Third Avenue
  New York, New York 10022

RELIGIOUS DEVELOPMENT IN CHILDHOOD AND ADOLESCENCE
Fritz K. Oser, W. George Scarlett (eds.)
New Directions for Child Development, no. 52 (Summer 1991)

ERRATUM

Page 1, line 1:

This sentence should read as follows: Everyone knows there are differences among the religiosity of children, youth, and adults.